birth | THE BIT IN
BETWEEN | *death*

THE BIT IN BETWEEN

birth | *death*

The Allure. The Taboo.
Living with Suicidal Depression.

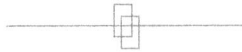

SINDA RUZIO-SABAN

Thanks to my brother
who has mostly been
a life-raft on stormy seas and,
to the best of his ability, helped make
the journey bearable.

Death is not the greatest loss in life,
it's what dies inside while we live.

—NORMAN COUSINS

———————————□——————————

Death can actually be a liberator. No matter how
reluctant we are to accept that.

—HENNING MANKELL

*I'd feel real trapped in life if I didn't know
I could commit suicide at any time.*

—HUNTER S. THOMPSON

| CONTENTS |

ACKNOWLEDGMENTS

M Y SINCEREST THANKS go to Laurel Ornitz (lornitza@comcast. net) who assisted in making my words more reader friendly and to Judy Abbate (www.abbatedesign.com) who created a book that is aesthetically pleasing and thus will hopefully bring pleasure to the eye as well as food for the brain while reading. Heartfelt gratitude to those of you who contributed with support, encouragement and friendship.

INTRODUCTION

Travelling is always like a children's game with its picnic
meals and makeshift sleeping places, its sense of having
escaped alike from past and future. She loved to journey
on, to adventure just a little further, to create afresh. She
could escape from herself best in those moments of vivid
experience that fresh scenes gave her.

—*Margaret Atwood*

First off, I am not a therapist, trained psychologist, or any other type
of clinician working in the field. Hence I do not come with years of
experience through observing hundreds of patients and this book is not
a result of years of research and study but is the outcome of a lifetime
of personal experience and learning. Rather than being a clinician's
observations from the outside looking in, it is a sufferer's view from the
inside looking out.

This was not conceived as a 'how-to' book but simply a sharing of
my personal journey with regard to lifelong chronic mild depression
interspersed with acute episodes as well as almost constant suicidal
thoughts and desires. There is also examination of the self-discovery that
has helped me cope with, if not totally cure, my malaise. I choose to share
this personal journey with you in the hope that some of my insights, my
toolbox, and the connected feeling of realising you are not totally alone
may help you. Also that through this you will discover ways that assist you

to continue your life's journey in a positive way. This is my desire and dream for you.

It is my hope some of my book will strike a chord – a chord that will help you discover your own voice, your own path, and thus give you the ability to lead your own life – not the life your mother, father, teacher, society, or the squirrels in your head say you *should* lead, but the one that your skin feels comfortable around. Having said that, trying to figure that out is a difficult path all its own – one I am still staggering along at this point! Who am I? What do *I* really want?

First and foremost is my desire to let you know you are not alone with your negative thoughts and feelings as for years I felt so incredibly alone with my suicidal thoughts. Admittedly, I often still feel this way, as it continues to be difficult to talk about them without feeling some measure of shame, without a degree of protection for others who fear this knowledge, as well as a measure of, perhaps, being accused of crying wolf when I am still here on this earth at fifty-nine! But on the other side of the scale I am convinced that the more I (we) talk the easier it becomes for all: sufferers, family, friends.

The discovery that keeping depression at bay is a lifelong task, there is no Shangri-La, was, and frequently still is, hard to accept. However, that daily commitment to well-being is the key for me, although often difficult to execute. This is where the 80 percent/20 percent rule helps and stops the perfectionist getting her whip out (i.e., if I am doing what I consider beneficial 80 percent of the time that is OK).

Although this book tells about my life and experience with chronic depression, my primary reason for wanting to write it was to bring suicidal thoughts out of the closet. Depression has almost become commonplace dinner conversation, and though that has helped lots of people recognise it and get help or be able to cope with or even assist friends suffering from depression the sometimes but not always companion to depression of suicidal thoughts is still taboo. Bring this topic up and heads avert, silence ensues, or a forced smile and some joke.

Come on! Let's talk about suicidal desires. Let's share these deep, dark, naughty thoughts. Let's drag suicide kicking and screaming from the deep well of our being and expose this beast. Bring it into the open where the light of knowledge, understanding, and, yes even, hopefully, acceptance of these desires (if not the actual act) will put it into its place – submissive *not* dominant.

There is also the fear that if we talk about it others may get ideas. Let me tell you I didn't (don't) need a handbook to come up with ideas. I read in a paper about the dangerous effects of aspirin overdose and filed that away ('Oh, if I take them, even if found, I can't be saved!' [This information was from years ago before dosages of many over-the-counter medicines have made them less 'effective']), or there is a warning about people who have died in a tent because they tried to keep warm with their gas stove ('Mmmm, didn't know that those tiny stoves could do that'). Recently I watched a gangster film in which there was a scene where someone was attempting to commit suicide with a car exhaust. I had always half rejected this idea as too complicated, having to get a hose big enough to fit the exhaust, affixing it, etc., etc. Oops, unintentionally the movie showed me how to do it easily. And let's not forget the Internet where with no effort all sorts of ideas can be found. So don't tell me that by being honest and open and talking about it I will get ideas. I can get them from anywhere and the secrecy only adds to my shame.

As indicated above, despite the oft-espoused view that talking about suicide may encourage others, it is my firm belief, through my own experience, that by keeping it locked away in the cupboard more harm is done. The more I talk about my suicidal thoughts the more I release them. Release them to be normal, not scary, not naughty, not anything other than a thought. A thought such as 'I like chocolate' or 'What a pretty flower'. This doesn't necessarily turn the thought into something benign nor necessarily lessen the desire at the time but it lessens the feeling of it being something bad and hence me being wicked.

By forcing suicidal thoughts and feelings into the background, they gain strength – the guilty secret feeding upon itself until the secret becomes part of the pain.

For me, the guilt and shame associated with feeling this way was intensified by the perception that I was the only one who seemed to lack the ability to enjoy life. The constant self-questioning of why couldn't I truly laugh and be excited like my family, my friends, others around me? Walking hand-in-hand with the loneliness was also the feeling of being naughty, of being a bad person for not enjoying life and for wanting to end it. These feelings exacerbated by the feeling of not having anywhere to turn.

> I felt I couldn't share my pain.
> I felt I couldn't share my despair.
> I felt no one would be interested.
> I feared they would use this intimate information to make fun of me, to ridicule me.
> I feared they would think me silly/stupid.
> I feared they would think I was a coward for not killing myself.
> I feared I would be taunted for trying to get attention.
> I fear I would be accused of trying to 'get the sympathy vote' as I was when I cried.

Of course, just to put a cherry on the cake, there was the guilt. On the one side: shame that I felt like killing myself. On the other side: guilt for not having the courage to do so. In the middle stood the child – hollow, smiling. This is not to say that once I opened the closet door and exposed suicide these thoughts disappeared. However, by sharing that I had them, and despite their continuing presence, they seem to have less power.

Later in this book, I talk about various ways I have found to help me to live with the 'black dog'. These are my solutions and are given as ideas or a starting point. We are all unique and will experience depression and suicidal thoughts differently so ways of coping will be as individual as our experience of it.

When I was younger, I used to write down things that spoke to me from other authors. This was until I discovered my own voice, although I still note those external verbal arrows when they hit a chord. Thus this book is a collection of my poems and diary entries mingled with extracts from other authors. All of this interspersed with remembered emotions that prompted my initial outpourings as well as reflections and evaluations.

My poetry is mainly written in the raw emotion of the moment. It comes unbidden, pours forth to be tinkered with later. The prose is a considered evaluation of how I felt (or my memory of how I felt) and how I believe these emotions came to be; it is reflective of the past as well as fleshing out the emotions contained in the poems.

I found (find) writing to be not only a great relief from the build-up of emotion, an emotional equivalent of lancing a boil, but over the years it has also been helpful in charting my patterns of behaviour and my emotional actions and reactions. Patterns unfortunately often repeated, but had I not kept some sort of journal, they are patterns I would not have been aware of. My scribblings are extremely sporadic, nothing like a daily or even weekly 'Dear Diary' – they are just a 'when I'm in that space' jottings. Nor do I suggest this is everyone's solution but it is something I have found helpful, as mentioned, both at the time of writing and for later consideration.

As a child I did not know about depression (nor that suicidal thoughts and depression are mostly cosy bedfellows) or even that what I was experiencing could have anything to do with being depressed – it was simply not talked about.

Not knowing I was sick I did not I know there was help at hand. I was aware only that I lived in almost constant emotional pain. I didn't want to be alive. When Mum would come out with 'You should be grateful for what I do', my only thought was that I didn't ask to be born and I am certainly not grateful for being alive so why should I be grateful for what you do? It was your choice to have me. So there.

Death wishes were a daily companion. I was somehow not able to stop myself spending hours fantasising about ways and means. Then not doing anything because I was fearful of negative outcomes. Eeek, waking up in a hospital bed. A failure! These feelings were closely followed by shame for not killing myself, for being so weak, so cowardly. Yet another failure!

This was a deliciously painful double-edged sword. Shame and guilt for wanting to kill myself. Shame and guilt for not killing myself. This shame and guilt exacerbated when a cousin attempted suicide, unsuccessfully as it happens, but at least she had the courage of her convictions, or so went my thinking!

> They were not attempting to understand me; so I took refuge in silence and odd behaviour. I wanted to make myself impervious to my surroundings.
>
> *—Simone de Beauvoir*

Increasingly, I felt more and more alone. I felt weird. Because I felt weird (unloved/ unlovable?). I ostracised myself by my cool exterior. A cool exterior that hid an inner neediness. My feelings of being unloved, and unlovable, increased with each perceived rejection. With hindsight I have to emphasise the perceived part of these rejections. However, perception being fact, I pulled further and further away from intimacy. I felt terribly alone, often even more so when surrounded by people, including family. Family in this case being my mother and brother – the rest scattered around the globe.

The feeling of being different, weird probably intensified by us (our mother, my brother, and me) moving from one end of the earth to the other and hence customs, language, friends, and anything familiar not once but twice before I was five! I learned and forgot Swiss-German and English twice in that time. For years I used to joke about the fact that there was a record (before the days of tapes, iPod, etc.!) made with me speaking when I was a child, it had been made to send to my father, and the adult me could not understand what the child me had said. In hindsight maybe it's not so funny?

How did these changes affect my feelings of being different? How did the constant upheaval add to feelings of insecurity? How did the feelings of being different add to the feelings of isolation? Was this the reason the child became wary of getting close to people, of making friends? Who knows but once in Auckland (NZ) the nomadic lifestyle didn't end as we moved homes many times. I attended three different primary schools and in fact where I am presently living (nine years) is the longest I have been in one home – ever.

An already insecure world was forever changing underneath me – if we don't move continents we move homes. Fathers go. So why bother with friends when the pain of parting was assured? Yes, I suppose I did have friends, playmates, but deep attachment was avoided. I was, and am, ever ready for the bond to be broken, so often appear cold and unfeeling when it occurs. My tears are, and ever were, private.

So back to the immense relief when I found out I was not alone with negative feelings, not alone with suicidal thoughts. The relief of discovering I was not weird or in any way *that* different from many others. The realisation was not an instant cure, I admit, but simply the start of a long, sometimes exhilarating, often painful, journey. A journey that continues to this day and will hopefully continue into the foreseeable future.

Unfortunately, realisation is merely the first step of many. The learning never ends. There is the initial pain involved in changing one's reactive behaviour to become proactive in one's own life and take responsibility for it. I tell you, as soon as I begin to think 'Ah ha, I've got it', along comes my next test! I don't fail all the tests and it is affirming to realise that some of my healthy behaviour is now automatic but there still seems a long way to go. Although the journey is ongoing and often arduous, the outcomes so far have been worth the effort, despite the occasional regression.

Then there is the positive of having found a measure of peace in myself and with others, most particularly family. Although our relationship was not suddenly all sweetness and light for all the 'I hate you's' uttered to Mum, I did reach a point of understanding and love with her. A place where I could accept that she had done her best, that it was now my life to live, and I was finally able to enjoy the good within our relationship. We even ended up going on holidays together. Holidays that were, mostly, fun to share! Hey miracles are few and far between, so old monsters did rear their heads now and again, but all in all I looked forward to spending time with her. Another plus of the making up, aided by the fact that we had warning that she was dying, was that when she died I was not left with the anguish of 'I wish I …'

Mum was bought up to succeed and with an immense sense of duty, doing what is right. Recently I was made acutely aware of that sense of duty. In a session my therapist said, 'OK, what if your mother had made her peace with God and was sitting up there looking down on you. What would she say?' Initially I said that she said she loved me. However, although initially Mum said, 'I love you', I realised that this was simply what the inner child wanted to hear. In fact she did not say this and the adult me had to accept that she would never say it or be able to give me love in a way meaningful to me. However, on continuing to sit with the emotion of the moment, I noticed she was crying. Mum's sorrow was real in that I could see and feel her sob and shake as she apologised for my pain, even though deep down she really didn't understand why I was in pain or what she had done to cause it.

Hadn't she done her duty and done it well? This led me to the realisation of how duty ruled her life, and hence ours. To her, by giving us good food, clothing, a warm bed, and the ability (often financial, at what cost to her one can only wonder) to follow our interests, sports, etc., she was being a good mother. A love so caught up in duty and obligation that it didn't feel like love. A love so layered by her having to prove herself to herself as much as to others that it didn't feel like love. But the pain of her sorrow for the anguish she caused me was so overwhelming that I had to pull back from this exercise. However, at the end of the day, this was a very constructive thing to realise as it provided another release of some of the old hurts and also helped me with some realisations about Dad's ability to show love.

With my father, the friendship has taken longer and is still a work in progress, the positive connection being relatively new. The benefit of my latest dip into the depths is that not only did he assist and support me in ways I could not have dreamed of but through our email conversations and my willingness to open up I have grown closer to him. I shared with him in an honest way. His responses were supportive and understanding, even though it occasionally took the old me, sometimes with help from my therapist, some time not to read negatives between the lines! Yes, I am still a little tentative and ready to be hurt but, with the buds of understanding opening, a gradual reconciliation within my heart is following.

While primarily about my feelings and our family, this book also explores the possibility of food, or even sex, as a substitute for the love we seek, the emptiness inside, the feeling of alienation. Then there is also the question of depression sapping all one's energy with this often being interpreted as being lazy, especially if one is only mildly depressed and hence to all intents and purposes functioning. If one doesn't even realise that one is depressed, how does constantly being told you're lazy when you don't seem to have any energy affect your self-perception?

But there is also a silver lining and there can be positives from living in this black cloud for most of the time. I am not saying depression and suicidal thoughts are a good thing and that I would rather not have lived my life with them but if one has to suffer why not explore some of the upsides, which I do, albeit briefly.

All in all at the end of the day and at the risk of being repetitive, I want to emphasise that my sincerest wish is that the sharing of my journey, my thoughts, and my discoveries along the way will be of assistance to you, be you a fellow suffer, someone who loves you (or tries to), or even someone just attempting to understand something totally alien. Let's face it, one often finds it hard to understand what one has not experienced but who knows when a friend or loved one or even a stranger may lean on you and with the insider's knowledge gained through my story you may at least feel comfortable.

PEOPLE

We share the same fears
We share the same insecurities

But we don't share our ownership of these

We strut
We puff
We put on a show

All false fronts

Anxious that the breeze of knowledge
will take these facades away

Leaving the inner

exposed

vulnerable

FIDN'T DIT

I don't fit
I can't fit
I didn't fit
I never fit
I won't ever fit
         a MIS-fit

Because I am odd people don't like me
But I don't know why I'm odd
Bloody hell
I don't even know what odd is!

a child's plea

Do love me – not in YOUR way but in mine
Do cuddle me – often
Do hold me – even when I'm not sick
Do notice me – not some reflection of your past
Do realise I don't make mistakes on purpose
Do be a little less efficient and a lot more loving

Don't leave me
Don't tease me
Don't make fun of me
Don't put me down
Don't hit me
Don't pretend to be perfect
Don't blame me for the bad parts of your life

a child's reality

My feelings of isolation, of not being loved, of not being loveable, who to share that with? A mother who didn't give love as I wanted? As I grew older, there was some awareness that Mum would have given up her life for me, but her life was not what I wanted. Being told 'I love you in my way' did not mean much when all I so desperately wanted was proof of her love. Proof shown in *my* way – a love I could understand. I wanted a love of softness, listening, accepting, praise, not one of teaching. Teaching meant constant criticism and need for improvement. The love I so desperately wanted was one of cuddles, laughs, understanding – not one of duty, obligations, and stern looks.

Then again, how to share any of this with a father who was distant not only in geography (him in Europe, us in New Zealand), but as my parents split up when I was four, I had no personal memory of him. The physical distance, exacerbated by a lack of contact, prevented any hope of being able to find mutual understanding, a connection, or perhaps even love there.

That is not to say all my memories are miserable but I lived in constant fear of being rejected *again*. My biggest rejection being my father leaving Mum (child's reality = me!), especially as he left not long after I was born. He'd stayed when my brother was born so it must be me. I convinced myself that it was because I was not good enough, not pretty, stupid, not a boy, and a myriad of other reasons. Whatever, at the end of the day, it didn't matter why, I just knew that it was my fault that he left.

It was also my fault that Mum couldn't marry again as no other man wanted me around. Therefore, clearly it was my fault that Mum was miserable. The adult now realises my parents' divorce and Mum not remarrying had little to do with me but the child only knew she had been rejected, been abandoned, and Mum's unhappiness was all the child's fault. It was my fault for not being ... well, to be honest, I didn't really know what I should have been, but I knew that whatever I was, it wasn't right.

So even though I knew I wasn't loved, I lived in constant fear of losing the only security I had. For me, the only way not to be abandoned yet again was to be what I believed the remaining parent wanted. This proved difficult as the rules kept changing but it did not stop me from evaluating every move, gesture, inflection of speech on the radar of acceptance, tolerance, and rejection. Unfortunately, my radar's wiring was programmed to prefer the rejection option and mostly continues to do so to this day. I have to be ever vigilant and questioning of others' intentions (when possible) to ensure I don't fall into the rejection equals worthless spiral.

I did not want to be on this earth while being told I should be grateful for everything my mother did. 'Huh? Me! Grateful? Why? I didn't ask to be born! You chose to have me so everything you do is just basically my right. Anyway, you don't love me, so doing what you consider your duty doesn't really count now, does it!' Thoughts only. Words never spoken. Not enough courage to give them voice. The fear (of what?) too great. As well as the nagging thought that as all Mum's pain was my fault maybe I did owe her something?

Being quiet (invisible?) may have kept me safe but also kept me in the jail of my thoughts. I became an avid reader, my escape from a reality I did not want to face. I continue to enjoy reading and accept it often continues to be an escape but also acknowledge that for me it is a vital portal to relaxation as well as information and that all are acceptable reasons to read (escape, relaxation, learning). I go through periods of devouring detective novels and thrillers, then informative or self-help books. Hey, I sometimes even do some of the exercises in the self-help ones. Whatever, I always had and continue to have a book at hand. The big gain for me is that I no longer feel guilty when reading, a huge step forward as to sit and read was considered being lazy. Mum was all action, do, do, do, and if we didn't do, do, do, we were lazy. I have slowly learned to be comfortable to be a human-being rather than a human-doing, but it took time and is a work in progress.

Both parents originated from Croatia and although family was scattered around the globe, none came this far south (we emigrated from Switzerland to New Zealand). I say none but actually Mum had a half-sister here when we arrived but they left soon thereafter never to return so it felt like no other family was here. So not only did I not have the balance of a father, I also lived far away from any relatives who may have brought some alternative perspective, or at least somewhere to run to catch my breath, or even just the companionship of others as 'weird' as us (funny food, accent, traditions, etc.). My feeling of loss with regard to relatives is recent and comes from the softening effect I note relatives sometimes bring to families. No I'm not delusional enough to believe it is always all sweetness and light but even if the family is bickering there seems to be some alternative view or attitude provided. For us, it was Mum's view and Mum's only, with her word being law.

I was made even more aware of the realisation of this loss of alternative standpoints when I travelled to meet relatives from both my mother and father. This time I limited them to close relations (first line of defence as I called it) as in the past the sheer volume of cousins x or y times removed proved overwhelming. Although I had met them before, on this occasion it was with a view to talking to them about family. The most interesting fact for me was the different perspectives they bought to their youth, their views of family members (for me, the main interest was my mother and father, of course) and life in general. Quite an eye opener and made me yearn for the possibility of relations living close – be they loved or hated!

Nor were there many friends to suggest the possibility of a different reality. Mum had few and we were not encouraged to bring any home. It was us against this alien, backstabbing world. They were out to get us and we had to stay strong and unified against this threat whatever that was! Don't let's even go down the track of the misery and teasing from other children (and some adults!) of having a mother with a 'funny' accent, and the weird foods we ate! Who had even heard of sauerkraut, liver sausage, or pumpernickel bread, yet alone ate it! (We emigrated in the 1950s.) Thus my feelings of isolation increased in so far as I felt an outsider both inside and outside of the home. Oh how I longed to fit in. Anywhere.

I lost any sense of self, not even being able to really decide what I was feeling or what I wanted so used was I to fitting in. However, it was not until I commenced therapy that I became conscious of this loss of *me*. In fact most of the initial sessions were spent becoming aware of me. Listening to that inner voice rather than the ones around me. In the past, I would agree to almost any thought, feeling, activity if it meant I fitted in, if I was (felt) accepted. It didn't necessarily feel comfortable, but it was what I knew, and fear of rejection kept me in this cycle. Although it may have been painful, years of honing this skill made it the easier option, with those first baby steps to being myself difficult and painful. *Difficult* and *painful* are words I can use to describe a lot of the work of changing old, known, but not good-for-me patterns. To this day it is still sometimes difficult to be me but fortunately I am now more aware when I play the fitting-in game and admit that there are times when it may be appropriate for me and my emotional health to fit in. The difference now it is often, but certainly not always, a conscious choice rather than an acquired, painful, and self-destructive habit.

Mum came from a dynastic background and pre-war lived in a very feudal society. She was born to immense privilege, to rule, with all the positives and negatives that this entailed. The war radically changed this landscape, not only taking her country but her way of life and any expectations of what her future would be like. As both parents came from wealthy and powerful families, neither Mum nor Dad were brought up with the expectation that they would work in the way that most of us understand that word, i.e., 9 to 5. It's not to say that aristocrats don't work, but when they do it is mostly in very different ways than the herd.

So along comes the war. During the war Mum was instrumental in her own high risk. Officially working for the Germans, she was an informer for her country, helping to sabotage bauxite shipments and ensure the release of prisoners. When her activities became known and confronted by the reality of being on the Gestapo List, her German Wehrmacht boss aided her to get by train to Triest, from where she proceeded on foot to Switzerland to reunite with her fiancé, our father. (How brave. A regular Mata Hari. Yet another impossible to live up to.)

They married, had us two children, but eventually the marriage failed. So came the divorce. Divorce in an era when this was not acceptable. Couples stuck together through thick and thin. Top that off with having been brought up a staunch Catholic and one can only imagine how traumatic this was for my mother. Add to this Mum's perfectionism and, if Mum's emotions after the divorce were anything equal to mine after my divorce, she would have felt a huge sense of failure. Failure! A total anathema to her expectations of herself and, unfortunately, of her children.

Quite apart from her own emotional standpoint with regard to divorce, society in the 1950s looked down on divorced women; men thought they were fair game and women would often assume the single woman was after their husband, so having friends of either sex was fraught with difficulty. Actually the latter viewpoint is something that I continue to come across as a single woman now but it was certainly more pronounced in the 1950s. The construct being that everyone wanted to be married – didn't they? Then there was the issue of sex, which outside of marriage was frowned upon, so to get it one had to be married, add to that the fiscal limitations for a woman on her own, so to have decent income, she needed a husband.

However, if we tap into Mum's feeling of failure for the moment, we, her product and evidence of her abilities, had to be more than perfect. She drove us no harder than she drove herself, but that didn't make it any easier – failure was never an option. Conversely, we were also a convenient excuse for any possible errors made by her; if a tap was left dripping, it was always one of us; if there was a miscommunication with directions, it was always us who hadn't listened; if we knocked over a glass (as children invariably do), we were clumsy and not paying attention even though she may have placed it by our side without our being aware of it.

So with the war Mum had not only lost her expected future life but she also lost her country (going back to Communist Yugoslavia does not appear to have been an option; I never queried why not). Then she lost the only man she ever truly loved (or so I believe) and ended up a divorcée, something not socially acceptable. Don't forget she came from a society where appearances were everything so to lose her status must have been devastating. Through the divorce, she became a refugee again and was not able to remain in Switzerland. Who knows why she chose the other end of the globe as her new home, a backward country with a culture that she did not have much in common with. One can only imagine how traumatic the combination of all this must have been and how it affected her. There was the added fact that Mum was a prickly person, difficult to be friends with (had she always been or did she become so through life's experiences?) and I am not unconvinced these factors didn't play a part in her keeping her distance and hence isolating us.

Did she move so far to be assured that Dad played no role in our lives? If that was her motivation, it worked. Perhaps not from any lack of desire on his part, although as a child I always believed this was the case, but more due to the constraints of communication at that time and the fact that, in my experience anyway, few children enjoy writing letters. Also by the time I was actually old enough to write anything meaningful any chance for connection had long since passed. Our interaction was stilted and formal and between the lines misunderstandings (on my side) plentiful.

This lack of a father, quite apart from feeling abandoned, precluded me from the possibility of feeling special in a father's (a man's) life, as daughters mostly are, and I feel my relationships with men have all been coloured by this massive need to feel special to a man. A need too massive to fulfil and so inevitably it ends up by me feeling rejected. The pundits continually say that fathers are essential role models for boys, yet I can't get away from the feeling they are also important for girls, providing the first man to whom they can feel special, cherished and maybe even beautiful. Put simplistically, if we are lucky, we learn our homemaking skills from our mothers and our man-woman relationship skills from our fathers. Settle down you feminists; this is not to say women are only homemakers but we do learn womanly things from our mothers, at whatever end of the feminist spectrum they may sit. I know I make mention elsewhere in this book of the devastation to children from divorce and I make no apologies for repeatedly attempting to show the effect it has on children, no matter their outward appearance.

If my mother's story is to be believed, Dad was absent through much of her pregnancy and at the event of my birth. So if Janov's (*The Primal Scream/The Feeling Child*) theory is correct and Mum was in emotional pain for most of her pregnancy with me, this pain would transfer through to me. Hence, was I born an emotional cripple? Was her pain, and blame (?), really transferred to me? Of course, I don't know but I do know smiling over pain is automatic for me. Mum always said I came out (meaning of her womb) smiling and have smiled ever since. Over the years, to my own detriment, I became an expert at hiding the pain with that smile and unfortunately still do. Despite all my insights and changes to self, when I hit bottom recently and was left staring at those walls, friends said, 'But I had no idea'.

TO WHOM IT CONCERNS

You are
   useless
   worthless
   irrelevant

You are
   a blight
   a fright
   a disgrace

However,
   I might
   I might
I just might love you ..... *if*

'If what'
   I scream
      silently

Too scared to hear
confirmation of an impossible ..... *if*

Too scared to affirm
I will never achieve ..... *if*

Easier
   not to know
   not to try,
   while all the time trying

every gesture
   every look
 every breath
      silently screams

LOVE ME

Please

WORDS

Words
sharper
more cutting than a Samurai sword
decimate me

Leaving
an outer shell
solid
strong
holding together
scuttling, bumping, jangling atoms
tortured, agonised fragments
of
my being

Words
scattered carelessly about
sparkling like diamonds
But
like diamonds
sharper than any blade

A cut stops bleeding
The wound heals
Sometimes
leaving a scar to tell its tale

Words
thrown out in an instant
stay implanted
sharp edges
continually reopening old wounds,
wounds never given time to heal

No scar to reveal the inner pain
A smile hiding the anguish
Silence concealing the torture

Words
feed the mind
but
kill the soul

AN EMPTY VESSEL

You died long before your physical death
Leaving a void inside yourself
left us nothing to find.

Creep, crawl, squirm, grovel, twist, turn.
Do what we may
you remained inviolate … unobtainable

A shell.
A beautiful, strong, capable shell.
Dr Spock★ would have been proud
of your intelligent lack of emotion.
Logic rules!

What place a heart?
How to feel an emotion?
How could you share what you did not have?

What right
to birth two children
with no means of caring.

We're children NOT ornaments
Cleaned. Dusted. Positioned.
Back on the shelf
Till next showing.

★Dr Spock of *Star Trek* fame, not the children's doctor popular in the 1950s

LEARNING

Why
when there is learning to be done
it is always I who must learn from you?

Do I really know so little?
Is what I know so foolish?
Or of such little worth?

Have I really nothing to offer the world
except crazy ideas, extremes, and black moods?

Surely
some of what I think is right?
Perhaps some of what I do could be right?

Not right
in the sense of right
       or
          wrong
       but acceptable
       or interesting
or possibly
just possibly
  I offer
    something
       you could learn from me?

| CHAPTER 2 |

suicide daydreams

All I want to do is to go to sleep and
never wake up again.
                                    —*Simone de Beauvoir*

Am I
sick and tired
of being
sick and tired
or just
of being
                                    —*Sinda Ruzio-Saban*

I AM FULLY AWARE that this is a taboo subject and frightening to many but I am also firmly of the opinion that *not* talking about it is more harmful to those of us who harbour these fantasies. Nor do I condone or condemn suicide and I am sure everyone who attempts or succeeds has their own reasons. I am writing of suicide and its allure for me in an attempt to bring suicidal thoughts and desires into the open, to expose suicide's power and attraction, give it light, and perhaps exposure will lessen its power for others just as talking more openly about it has lessened its power for me?

I categorise my suicidal experiences into active and passive. Active is where I am seriously planning or even attempting suicide; passive is where I just wish a bus would run me over. Mostly when I come out at the end of the long black tunnel or climb out of the deep pit of depression, I am, for a time, split: one side of me beginning to see the sunlight and wanting to engage in life again, while the other remaining in the passive suicide role – rocking easily and swiftly from one side to the other.

I spent, and admittedly continue to spend, a lot of my time planning various scenarios of how I would kill myself. The main criteria, no pain. Which when looked at logically is really rather amusing as more often than not when I dream of escape I am in so much pain would any extra really matter?

For much of my youth I was considered ditzy in that I would end up stepping into the road in front of cars or buses with my mind apparently elsewhere. I certainly didn't do it with any conscious intent, but in hindsight I wonder if this was a form of subconscious passive suicide? Don't forget I was not aware I was suffering from depression or that my wish for death could almost be classified as normal for this disease. Back to almost being run over, I need to stress that in all my fantasies I don't involve anyone else. I feel the guilt at running someone over, even if that person wanted to be run over, must be awful and some sense of fairness prevents me from involving others. But perhaps my subconscious had a different ethic.

Being haunted, almost continuously, by feelings of wanting to escape life even on the good days made me feel I was bad, that there was something wrong with me. I saw everyone else as enjoying life and I just couldn't seem to. *'What is wrong with you?'* *'For goodness sake, snap out of it!'* *'You're not really trying.'* *'Get a grip'* the tape in my brain looped constantly. I was ashamed of my thoughts. Was this shame of even my thoughts another reason for my rabid need for privacy? What was even worse and increased my shame was that I didn't seem to have the courage to actually carry any of these scenarios out. There was a sort of an internal dare that took place and I felt worse each time I seemed to wimp out by finding an excuse for not killing myself. Shame that I so desperately wanted to die yet seemed too cowardly to do anything about it (my first attempt was not until I was in my early twenties).

Guilt was also my constant companion. I felt guilty because everyone else seemed happy. They appeared to look life straight in the eye whereas I always felt I could only glance at life for small moments before the pain was too great and I felt obliged to turn away. Oh yes, I was fun – the proverbial joker. While the outside of me laughed and joined in, inside there was a constant thrust of knives, arrows, and sharp instruments cutting and slicing. The shame and guilt building on itself, as well as any perceived slight or rejection adding another knife. A vicious cycle. I felt bad for wanting to kill myself and then felt even worse for not doing so. This lack of conviction and/or courage just added to the plethora of reasons I could think of why I was unlovable. A poor excuse for a human being really.

When younger, my desire for death was mostly to escape the pain of lovelessness, the feeling of being redundant in this world, of being not good enough, the belief that I was superfluous to requirements. Admittedly, there was also a tinge of hope that '*You'll be sorry when I'm gone.*' '*When I'm gone, then you'll see what you couldn't see while I was here!*' Recognition at last! Much as I wanted to get rid of the pain, I also hoped to make them suffer. Suffer as much pain as they had made me suffer but, if I'm honest, tinged with a smidgen of hope that their pain would be greater.

As I grow older, it is not so much the emotional pain that causes me to wish I were no longer on this earth but a general questioning of 'What is it all about' 'What, if any, is my relevance?' 'Is this as good as it gets, and if so, why continue to struggle on?' Becoming invisible (age does that for you, just wait!), the body slowly wearing down, the growing physical pain added to the emotional one, all cause me to increasingly ask, 'What's the point?' In youth, there is the hope that things will get better. As I age and the span of time for this improvement to happen decreases, the window of hope reduces correspondingly. Those even older than me say it only gets better but as the roller coaster continues I often wonder.

Unfortunately, although I am aware of it being to the detriment of my happiness in the here and now, I continue to forget to acknowledge what is and tend to concentrate on what could be. This is where daily, or even more frequently, an Attitude of Gratitude is of great help. To notice the small positives, take time to watch a bee bumbling along, my cats playing with each other, the lovely warmth of a hot shower on a cold day.

The bottom line is that while I have acquired tools to help me appreciate life it continues to be a daily vigilance against the blackness. I have had to accept that I will never be cured and that this is OK. I concede I have never been, nor likely to be, I feel, one of those people who wakes up greeting the day with gusto, enthusiastically glad to be alive. But having gathered tools that when used enable me to appreciate the good and help the battle with the bad, I created a life that is at the very least liveable and on occasion even one to enjoy.

In the overall scheme of things and given a choice I would rather not be inclined to depression and suicidal feelings, but as that doesn't seem an option for me, I seek the positive. Weird as it may sound suicidal musings often help keep me alive through the pain.

MY FAITHFUL FRIEND

My faithful friend
you kept me alive
through all those years
of barren wastelands
and Arctic winds

'I love you *in my way*'
meant but little to the one
whose *way* was so different from yours
the gulf too wide for any connection to be made

Loneliness

Solitude

But, my faithful companion
you waited patiently to comfort
when no comfort was to be found
to give hope
in the mire of hopelessness

You are there still
Silent as ever
but
should the pain overpower
should I lose all shred of light
You will provide the ability
the strength
to achieve my heart's desire

My dear, dear fantasy friend
more true than any flesh and blood
when others deserted me
you kept me alive

Dear.   Sweet.   Faithful.
Suicide daydreams

MY LOVE

I sit
in the middle of
the field of broken dreams

The realisation of all my fantasies
nestled in my hand

Not bright and shiny
as always imagined
but
     dull
        and
           black

So Small
So Insignificant.
to be
So Final.

I stare at you
as I stroke your smooth surface
extolling in your cool feel
my finger traces your curves
enjoying your symmetry
luxuriating in your solid strength
your cool hardness
velvet on my lips
nectar on my tongue

My saviour
I devour you with all my senses
cradling and caressing you
loving you for enabling me
to erase my pain

Now all I ask is
the courage
the strength

to
 pull
   the trigger

| suicidal thoughts and fantasies |

Seeking perfection in life
I seek the perfect death.
What is the perfect death?
How can I be sure it will be the perfect death?
There is no ability to trial

—*Sinda Ruzio-Saban*

My biggest *if only* in times of thoughts of suicide has always been 'If only I had a gun', other methods not only not giving the same illusion of guaranteed success, but also I don't know how painless they really would be. Mind you, I'm not sure how painless shooting myself would be, but in the fantasy, it is quick and painless. As I twist in my cage, I continue to seek the *perfect* suicide – chatter, chatter, chatter …

'If I take tablets, when I fall asleep, do I feel any physical pain? Do I truly slide into a sleep and doze though all the destruction in my body? Or do I lie racked in pain while the pills do their slow work of destruction. Is it fast? Or does it all take a long time? How many tablets to make it *really* fast and certain? Mmmm, with tablets I could be found, rescued. Oh *no*! A gun in the roof of my mouth is instantaneous and painless … surely?! Yes, it requires courage to put it there and pull the trigger but that done the rest is clear … surely?!'

'BANG! The last sound I hear. As I hear it, the bullet enters the brain, shattering it, and instantaneous and, more importantly, painless.'

'If I electrocute myself in the bath, what happens? Do I feel burning? Does my heart thump painfully? Do I spasm? Am I acutely aware of the electricity running through my body until my heart, lungs, brain (whichever) packs in first? Or do I simply become unconscious and drown?'

'How long would I free fall if I jumped off a high building? Would I be aware of any pain? Is it possible to land in such a way so as to die slowly, lingeringly, or worse still not to die at all!'

The poem 'What If' is basically a summary of my various suicidal musings with the following texts expanding my fantasies around various options.

WHAT IF

What if I could
  stop breathing
    cut my wrists
      put a gun to my head
        take too many tablets
          sit in a warm bath and throw in an electric heater
        jump off the harbour bridge
      crash my car into a brick wall
    eat myself to death
  vanish

What if I
  stop
    bleed
      shoot
        overdose
          electrocute
        jump
      crash
    explode
  ...

What if

SHOOT MYSELF DAYDREAMING

Wonder how I can get a gun. Good start would be where from!

I imagine this lovely small gun. It fits snugly into my hand. Maybe with a pearl handle as I've read about. Hopefully a small gun would be powerful enough to do the job?

Or should I do a Clint and 'Make *my* day'. Well it would certainly be making mine! How big is a Magnum whatever? Not sure if I like the thought of a really big gun. Oh well can't get one so what's the point even thinking about it.

How I wish I were in the States where, by all accounts, guns appear to be easy to get. Such a hassle here. Such a palaver to actually get one. Mind you, if I had the right contacts, I suppose I could get one, but don't know anyone in the criminal world. Huh imagine going up to a Black Power headquarters and asking to buy a weapon. Get back to reality girl! Suppose I could get one in a gun shop. But would I then have to join a gun club? Still if I did I would then at least know how to load the damn thing. Probably useful to know so I don't mess it up! Don't need to be a good shot though do I!

Would across the temple be best?
Or in the mouth and through the top of the head?
Been told neither is guaranteed but *really* how can you blow part of your head off and live?

Must be untrue.

Mind you, if I turn out a vegetable, my pain will still be gone so no problem?
But then again I'd be a burden for those remaining.

Oh hell and damnation of course it would work!
It *must* work

Off
Out

Into a secluded field

BOOM

silence

joy?

> *I had this daydream more when I was younger when much as I wanted to end my pain hurting Mum was also a part of it all.*

SLIT WRISTS DAYDREAMING

The cross on the forehead.
As the blood seeps out from the cuts, I can almost feel the crook of Mum's little finger on my forehead, as she balances her hand, enabling her to make the sign of the cross with her thumb.

Then the quick kiss where the cross had been formed followed by the distanced goodbye.

It's the only time I remember Mum kissing me or touching me gently when I was not sick.

The memory causes tears to run down my cheeks, my face now coursed with rivers of dark red interspaced with these sparkling jewels.

The 'good-bye' cross.

As this is the last journey I intend to take, I enjoy using this symbol, in defiance, and in the pain of the memory that this is all the tenderness I can recall.

I leave no suicide note – the cross is my farewell.

Slowly my face disappears as steam from the bath mists up the mirror.
The ache in my chest draws me to the warm womb of the bath.
As the warmth envelopes me, I lean back and briefly enjoy feeling warm and caressed and secure.
Now for the second step.

I know not to cut across the wrists. Now *that* would only end in the humiliation of waking in a hospital bed.

I slash the length of one lower arm,
and quickly,
before I am unable
the other.

Slowly I watch the clear water turn from clear to light pink,
from light pink to dark pink,
from dark pink to light red,
from light red to ever darkening red ....

PILLS DAYDREAMING

I walk from shop to shop buying a packet here, a packet there, just in case buying multiple packs in one chemist causes suspicion.
Still what could they do? Better safe than sorry.
'Head down girl, remain as invisible as possible, and just focus on getting a supply.'

Gosh, I hope that what I read was true.
NO MATTER WHAT these pills will so damage my liver, or was it the kidney or perhaps the stomach?
Who remembers?
Does it matter?
Who cares which?
Because, because, because, because
HA, even if they do find me and pump me out, I will have the final laugh.
I will be so internally damaged survival is impossible.
But is what I read true?

Mind you, I read that article so long ago, have they changed the formula?
Hopefully not. Bloody hell, how embarrassing if it doesn't work.

Why oh why don't I have the guts to get some sleeping pills? Would a doctor really ask such awkward questions? It would be easier, wouldn't it? Surely they must work. But then again they've probably changed the formula of them too by now. Would sleeping pills be easier anyway? Nah not necessarily and who knows where *that* request to a doctor would lead. Keep your misery to yourself girl.

I wonder how many is enough?
Will they be hard to swallow? Well I suppose a few at a time should be OK.
Will I lose consciousness before I have taken enough?
Oh please NOOOOO, no, no, no – I am NOT waking up in hospital.

Will they do the job?
Will it hurt? I may want to die but not in pain.
I want to get rid of my pain not cause me more!
Hopefully I will just fall into a blissful sleep, never to awaken.
Surely that is how it will go.
It must!

JUMP OFF BRIDGE DAYDREAMING

Yes, that's what I'll do. First put the suicide note in an obvious place. Have some rubbish food on the way – who cares about health now! I'll do it late at night. Not so many people. Less chance of being seen and things going wrong.

Also the darkness feels apt – going from dark to dark.

All I have to do is drive to the top of the Harbour Bridge. OK I know they have cameras and all that but surely it can't be *that* hard to succeed. All I have to do is stop, run quickly – well hop, skip, and jump really – to happiness. Basically speed is of the essence. By the time anyone knows what is happening, I'll be plummeting down to the feel of solid concrete that water can apparently become when experienced from a great height.

Wonder what it will feel like. Will I feel like I am floating? Or will it be just a fast descent? Wind rushing across my ears? Does the time go quickly or slowly I wonder?

Must remember not to instinctively perform a dive. Not sure if that would make a difference but the old belly flop from a low diving board hurt enough. Also I trust that if I lie flat there should be maximum, irreparable damage.

Still even if I manage to survive the fall, hopefully I should be knocked out so that my body's instinct to save me fails and I drown.

They, which they? Oh who cares.
They say from a height the water becomes like solid concrete and you can break lots of bones. Crushed lungs too perhaps? Whatever, I just hope it doesn't hurt too much. But then again drowning is supposed to be quite a pleasant experience so even if I remain conscious for a time it shouldn't be too bad.

Mind you, I do hope I die quickly. I want to avoid as much pain as possible. Pain, uh I should be used to it I suppose, but just cause I've had it all my life let's make death less agonising if possible ay?

Nah, think positive, it will be quick and there really is little chance of failure.

Note written.
Cats fed and cuddled.
Time to go.

| euthanasia |

Hope is the worst of evils for it prolongs the
torment of man.

—*Friedrich Nietzsche*

I know this is yet another topic that people argue about and you may
wonder why I choose to discuss it here, but, as with this book I am trying
to be honest about suicide and bring this into an open forum, I wanted
to bring my thoughts about euthanasia to the table as well.

During my latest brush with deeper suicide thoughts, I was reading
a book about euthanasia. A book written by an advocate of this as a
solution for terminally ill patients who don't want to fight anymore. What
got me agitated was that whilst the author was extremely supportive of
anyone with a terminal physical illness being allowed to find their own
solution, as soon as he touched on the topic of mental illness his view was
instantly negative.

Why?

What is the difference?

There are people who whilst they may be at exactly the same stage of
a terminal illness will fight till the bitter end yet others will just want to
give up. As it is with people who struggle with life. So what is so different
between physical and psychological illness?

It frustrates me that even to someone who is an advocate of euthanasia
a person with a mental illness is considered a piranha. Oh yes, a person
with a physical illness is allowed to give up. *That's* OK. But as soon as it
is psychological you *must* be cured. Why? Especially when the ability to

experience any pleasure at all, or see any pleasurable future, has continued for many years or, as in my case, for my whole life.

> To survive
> one needs to discover
> the elusive and fleeting emotions of
> HOPE
> DESIRE
> PASSION
> and if one doesn't
> is one to be condemned to a life of hell?
>
> —*Sinda Ruzio-Saban*

THIS SACRED LIFE?

Life must be preserved
at all costs you insist
All life is sacred you argue

What makes it so?
What of the life being preserved

A life of darkness
of pain
of misery
of endless corridors with doors closed

What is so precious about dark days, endless nights?
What about this agony is so sacred?
What about this despair needs to be preserved?

Is this a life really worth saving?
Have you thought of that?

or even whether
this person
whose life you hold so sacred
wants to be saved

| a positive aspect to suicide daydreams

As some of my poetry points out, the thought of suicide helped me through painful times and in its own way helped keep me alive. To repeat Hunter S. Thompson's quote at the beginning of my book, 'I'd feel trapped in life if I didn't know I could commit suicide at any time'.

Suicidal thoughts have caused me to seek out therapy, which is something that has helped me make some sense of my life, myself, and made it easier for me to live my life not only with more understanding and hence more fully but also with a modicum of pleasure. I don't wish to imply that suicidal thoughts are necessarily a positive thing but I have noted that for me they have not necessarily been all negative. If I (we) have to live with them, let's find the positive!

Suicidal thoughts mean that death doesn't frighten me. I don't remember ever having an imaginary friend other than my suicide daydreams. Daydreams that help me survive in this troubled world where my personal happiness seems to lie beyond my reach! It (death) to me is comforting. The thought that if life really does get too tough I have a means of escape has actually been a great support! Hence, ironically, dreams of death help to keep me alive.

Suicidal thoughts have given me courage, however false, to do things and take risks others shy away from or just not panic about old age and end up living in the future rather than now. I have never thought of myself as a risk taker but now, finally, I can hear others' statements of 'Gosh you're brave' or 'I'd never have the nerve to do that?' Not that I have gone mountain climbing, base jumping, or any of those adrenaline-rush type things but I've just been more likely to take a risk with relatively ordinary things like job change or moving to different countries without a backward glance. Without really thinking about it consciously, there was always the thought that 'If this doesn't work out, I can always jump off a bridge'. A thought that gave me a freedom I now realise others who fear death don't seem to have.

As stated, I would prefer not be inclined to depression and the associated suicidal desires but as I have not found a way to rid myself of them entirely, nor do I think there is a way for me to do so, I seek the positive.

While I have for some time been aware that not fearing death and thoughts of this escape have kept me alive, the recent slightly longer period of depression, a certain ennui about the future (helped perhaps by my age) and the thought that I could at any time opt out have also given me a modicum of peace with my present situation. The constant fear of getting old and retirement, while I am not totally immune, is mitigated by the fact that if it all turns to custard and I am on the bones of my arse I can exit, stage left, so to speak.

The question is, 'Would I ever have the courage to actually commit suicide?' At the end of the day whether I could or couldn't isn't relevant, as the belief that I could seems sufficient to help keep me going and only time will provide the answer.

trust / fear

I wish I hadn't become so conscious of everything, every little nuance. Once I wouldn't have noticed, now every conversation, every encounter with a person seems like crossing a mined field, and why can't I accept that one's closest friends at moments stick a knife in, deep, between the ribs?

—*Doris Lessing*

T RUST OF OTHERS for me meant letting go of the fear of being misunderstood, being ridiculed, being lied to, and a myriad of unfathomable fears. Also there was the need, which continues, to learn to trust my emotions, my instincts. For me to gain real peace there has to be an ultimate trust in my Higher Power/The Universe and belief that whatever happens to me has a purpose. Admittedly, this is a trust I struggle with, but when I am in that zone peace is my companion. Although it is not the only way I have ever gained peace, it has been the one through which I achieved the deepest contentment.

As a child, I felt my world was constantly changing. Quite apart from the fact that we moved not just homes or countries but ends of the globe, there was the added fact that I never felt sure of Mum's reaction or her mood or her rules, all of which seemed to change on a whim. Talk about shifting goalposts, it felt as if the whole field was being tilted – my world constantly tipping! What was OK one day was not the next. A minefield of eggshells scattered over glass shards to be negotiated.

Through constantly being told my thoughts, perceptions, feelings were wrong, or my feelings being dispensed with, I trusted no one, nothing, not even myself. I felt I lived in this oppositional world of warmth – a warmth that could abruptly change into Artic coldness. Warmth snatched away without warning or any rationale that this young mind could fathom.

There was also the pain of my feelings being negated. Who of us hasn't heard the 'I'm *not* angry' response to the question of 'Why are you angry?' Through these and many other similar instances of being told what I was experiencing was wrong, I learned not to trust even my feelings. Maybe the tight face, steely eyes, and clipped response weren't manifestations of anger? Did I misread the tense atmosphere? The child retreated into silence and doubt. It made the wooden spoon preferable in that at least then I knew Mum was angry, even if I didn't necessarily have any better idea of why. Physical pain recedes with time, the emotional one remains.

Even my own sadness was often mocked. Either it was 'That's nothing to be sad about' or as I blinked my eyes to hold back the tears it was 'Look at you, pumping out the tears. Well you won't get my sympathy that way'. The child remembers the agony caused by the injustice of this statement. I was trying so hard *not* to cry. The adult remembers the pain of not being allowed to show sadness. I still have difficulty crying in front of people as I fear they will see me as seeking the sympathy vote. In fact I have found the best place for crying is in the shower. I highly recommend it! I can make as much noise as I want and, mostly, not be heard. An added bonus is that the water washes away all the tears, snot, and other nasties that go along with crying, as well as the fact of standing under a hot shower is something I find extremely soothing. Lots of birds with one shower there!

OK, so I wasn't allowed to be sad or upset. What about happy or animated? Well, if I was excited about something, then I was showing off or being too loud. In the end the only safe emotion was to stay outwardly composed all the time. Mind you, even that had its pitfalls as then I was accused of being remote. Confusion reigned supreme. Confusion I couldn't share so building a moat around this castle continued to seem to be the best solution.

Living in my head had the advantage that Mum could not invade that space. Privacy was an alien word and I firmly believe Mum went through my belongings. When I returned from having been out, were things moved in my room? I couldn't be sure, but it certainly felt that way. For me proof that Mum snooped was that if she got the letters from the mailbox, letters addressed to me were accidentally opened and there was never much interest in what they contained. However, if I got to the mailbox first, I felt hounded until I shared what was in them. Absolute proof that unless I kept all my feelings and thoughts inside my head Mum would know everything! No 'Dear Diary' for me. Sometimes I felt I would burst with thoughts, feelings, desires, all unexpressed. The fear of ridicule, of being made fun of, of my feelings being disregarded to which was added the anxiety that anything shared might be made into humorous anecdotes for others' amusement kept me silent.

So here was my conundrum. I couldn't share with Mum, through fear of her negative reaction, the fear of my situation being made fun of, the fear of being told my feelings were wrong. I couldn't share with my father; he was too far away and anyway I felt he wouldn't understand, that he didn't care. Let's face it, he'd left me! Quite apart from his jokey responses to my letters that left me feeling misunderstood by and alienated from him. I couldn't share with my brother who I felt was on Mum's side anyway as he also teased me mercilessly. So the cycle came back to me, locked in the prison of my head.

They say you are as sick as the secrets you keep. Well all I now know is that until I started leaking with therapy I was a very sick puppy! Quite apart from the fact that until I did start talking I wasn't aware of how sick I was. Re(?) discovering what I felt. Sharing these feelings. Finding out what I wanted and how to express these wants. Bit by bit learning to be open with others was, and continues to be, a slow and often painful slog but the journey continues to be worth it. Unfortunately, there is no utopia or even an end, just a flattening of the peaks and troughs so the differential between the emotional highs and lows is not so great. The road may be full of twists and turns as well as being seemingly never ending but I have found there are enjoyable meadows and streams by which to rest and catch breath at along the way.

Just recently I was going to a mystic fair with some friends. They had decided to leave in the late morning. I happened to say that I normally chose to go early as I felt all the clairvoyants and tarot readers were sucked dry later in the day. They all responded with various versions of how this wasn't so and it was stupid to think that. I felt my inner child pulling back and the beginnings of a feeling of rejection and ridicule surfacing. Guess what? The adult me then asked them not to negate my reality. They tried to argue that of course the readers were still OK. With a pounding heart, I managed to say again, 'Don't negate my reality. That they are not sucked dry is your reality and by saying this isn't so you are rejecting my reality. I would accept you saying 'I don't believe they are sucked dry' but don't make it a fact that they aren't. Although they continued to make fun of what I thought, albeit subdued, I felt better for defending myself and my inner child grew a few inches. Will it change the way they react in the future? I don't know and that is unimportant. What is important is that every time I manage to stand up for myself (the inner child?) I get stronger at doing it. Sorry to say it's still a long way from easy though.

The above, and other smaller instances, may seem like a minor thing and I know I have often said to myself 'It doesn't matter' or 'Don't make a big thing of it' but you know what, it is important to me and the more often I stand up for myself in these minor things the better I feel about myself. The better I feel about myself the more able I am to stand up for myself in more important matters. Not to say that I bang on about everything. There are things that really aren't important enough, but the trick is to start to realise when I feel it is essential for me to make a stand and when not. As with everything, it is an ongoing process. I know I repeat this ongoing part of the learning but thinking I have *got it* is still one of the stones that trip me up.

TRUST

An emptiness
deep within
the pain achingly intense
a void full of nothing
yet overflowing with
the pain of
      loss
        guilt
       fear
        uncertainty

Where are you?
You, who can ease this?
What use seeking relief
Yet not daring to trust

'Relief is within' I'm told

The pain intensified
by the knowledge
I trust no one
not even
myself

INERTIA

I soar
I float
I spin
I twirl
    I fall

I soar with dreams
I float with desire
I spin with joy
I twirl with excitement
    I fall with fear

Fear
    reality
    logic
    being adult

Is fear the reason?
Is fear the excuse?

HELP

Surrounded
Cornered
Trapped

Surrounded by
        should'-s
        should not'-s
        must do'-s
        mustn't do'-s

Cornered by fear of showing
        vulnerability
        weakness
        wants

My much valued honesty
Trapped by my need to be
        capable
        strong
        good

does tiredness really equate to being lazy?

The whole day thus far has been an exercise in FORCING myself to do the tiniest things and trying to evaluate how serious my situation is. Am I really depressed? Am I just lazy?

—*Andrew Solomon*

TREACLE. SUCH A SWEET TREAT. Not for me it wasn't. My world felt full of this sticky, persistent goo. Every step a tough slog through this unyielding black mass. Each step an exhausting push against this ocean of glutinous stuff. Then there was the added tension of the minefield of where to place my foot so it didn't hit a hidden bomb, the detonating of which would create an explosion that could cause my world to blow up.

Every moment of each day lived with this anxiety was exhausting yet I was not allowed to feel tired. *That* was being lazy. Did Mum know this exhaustion could be a sign of depression? Was this the reason that she hated idleness? Was it her fear that kept the knowledge of this aspect of the family history from me? Was her constant need for activity her way of coping? Was this her way of running from her own black dog?

Not until years later did I look at her response to 'How are you?' in a completely different light. I admit 'Still alive' seemed a strange response but I never really examined it at the time. However, as I struggle daily with staying alive, I wonder if she too led a double life, one to show to the outside world and one inside her head? Did she in a perverse way overcome her exhaustion by keeping constantly active? Was any sign of weakness in me confronting her own and thus I was not allowed to provide this mirror. The exhaustion of depression rather than being acknowledged for what it was being labelled lazy? My mother's nickname for me of Princess not stemming from being special or for any positive reason but from my 'being a lazy bum and expecting everyone to run around for me'.

Although I am more comfortable these days with spending a day horizontal I still struggle with feelings of being lazy. The list of to do's runs an almost constant loop in my head and it has taken much effort to attain a reasonable level of ease with being idle. I need to remind myself that we are human-beings *not* human-doings.

Of course there is the added problem that then when I do things I tend to notice what I have *not* achieved rather than the other way around, another hangover from youth as what was missed was more likely to be pointed out than what was achieved. Yes, children do learn from being shown their mistakes but don't forget to praise what they have achieved. The balance between overindulgent praise and excessive criticism no doubt being as difficult as the rest of parenting but both are required to give the child a sense of self, of balance. Also accept that sometimes adults forget things and miss doing a whole job too so let your children know you're not perfect either.

Thus, it now takes a conscious effort for me to accept that (a) I don't have to be doing all the time and (b) I am not lazy. As a therapist pointed out, I need to remind myself of the seasons in nature where each has its place in the cyclical nature of life – and rest is definitely part of this cycle.

Being lazy is also a perspective, with my reality not necessarily being another's. Example: I was on a health retreat and the person in charge had analysed my walking and made recommendations to help alleviate some physical problems I have when power walking. The next morning I went for a longish walk trialling these suggestions. When we were talking later and I mentioned about being lazy, he pointed out that I was not lazy, using as an example that a lazy person would probably not have been walking anyway but if they did they would have filed the information with regard to walking away for use later but I went out and walked. Firstly I did not think of it that way as I felt I should have walked further or practised more! However, little pats on the back like this are golden, not only pointing out another perspective, they also help keep the negative talk at bay. Through learning the power of such affirmations I now try and share the pleasure around and give praise to others, without being gushing about everything someone does as I feel praise then loses value.

To assist reminding myself that I am not lazy I occasionally write down three things I have achieved that day. Unfortunately, I tend to mainly do this when I am slipping down the slope or have hit bottom and am crawling back up. However, as I am writing this, I make note to self that it could be useful to do it even when I am in a good space. Whatever. When I do write down my achievements, it elevates my mood and reminds me that I did do something that day. Otherwise I tend to focus on the lack of activity, what there is to do that has not been done. The achievement doesn't have to be big. In fact it was once pointed out to me that we forget to applaud the little things so I try to make a point of including them. Sometimes my achievement is as simple as cooking a meal. How can that be an achievement? Well firstly I did eat and secondly I didn't just open a can, a packet, or go out and get take-aways. With the added bonus that the home-cooked meal, hopefully, being a healthier option.

To further demonstrate to you how banal the list can be, here are a few examples from my latest brush with depression.

2 Sept 2007
did ironing
removed carpet from bottom stair (cat had been peeing there for some time!)
weeded for 15 min

3 Sept 2007
made healthy supper
phoned re hair appointment
listened to relaxation tape in a.m. AND p.m.

5 Sept 2007
got up (yes often this is an achievement in and of itself)
wrote up notes for therapist
did fun questionnaire from book

Being labelled, or feeling, lazy is even easier in today's world with the pressure to not only achieve but also constantly improve both at work and at play. Here in New Zealand, I'm not sure about elsewhere, when employed there are now regular (mostly six or twelve monthly from my experience) performance development reviews. Reviews in which we have to outline our goals, what course(s) we may want to take to either achieve these goals or simply to improve. As I once said to a manager, surely not everyone needs to constantly advance, we need the drones too? Yes it is positive that employees are now assisted by employers to advance their careers *if they wish,* but I don't feel it should be a requirement as not everyone wants to. Advancement is now almost obligatory and we happy drones are not left to be. We thus end up feeling inferior or that something is wrong with us or yes we are just plain lazy. Even without any formal reviewing, as carried out here in New Zealand, I am sure the pressure to constantly improve, to better your performance at work and play is worldwide.

Through the women's liberation movement, women now have more freedom to work in paid employment. The trouble with this particular freedom is that those who don't work in a paying job are left feeling inferior. I emphasise paying job but I do hope that no one really believes being a mother/homemaker is not work. However, despite a mother/homemaker being an essential part of society it is no longer considered acceptable to *only* be a mother/homemaker. If you are not paid for what you do, it doesn't seem to count.

Superman: Well he gets to save the world with accolades a plenty. Superwoman: Mmmm, she only gets exhaustion with a report card of *could do better*. Exhaustion from working at a demanding job where often the needs of children are considered an inconvenience or intrusion and then after a gruelling day she gets to go home, to cook dinner, to clean, to wash clothes, to …, to … Where once perhaps (?) there was some down-time, when the children had their afternoon nap, there now seems to be none for Supermum. (Before I have the Superdads complain, I point out that I use the title Supermum for ease and as it is still a role mostly left to the women.)

Oh, let's not forget that she has to be fit and slim, so the gym/exercise needs to be fitted into the timetable.

Thus if she is not achieving at all these levels she is considered, or feels herself to be, of lesser value as well as lazy, if not by others at the very least by herself.

Even in the bedroom she can no longer relax and just enjoy her partner or a good night's sleep. The constant barrage of how to improve your sex life creating an uncertainty about how well she is performing and perhaps what new tricks she should be trying. Even though she has just worked a full day, rushed from pillar to post dropping off and then picking up children, cooked a meal (healthy of course and only bad mothers buy take-aways), picked up the toys, done some washing, perhaps ironing too, or just guiltily rushed through the essential chores. A full-on day yet she's not allowed to feel too tired for a marathon sex session!

The sad thing for me about modern living perhaps aiding and abetting feeling tired or depressed is that I wonder if it is not a chicken and egg situation, i.e., 'I am constantly exhausted because I am depressed' or 'I am depressed because I am constantly exhausted by the expectations of modern life and the feeling of being a failure for not having the energy I (society) think I should have?' Are the expectations on us in modern society the base cause in the increase in depressive illnesses?

Another side of the perceived lazy coin is just plain not competing. My brother and I have the misfortune to come from a family where high achievers apparently abound. Why do I say misfortune? Well as a child all I remember hearing about was these great people who had influenced history, helped shape nations, were famous whatevers, yada yada yada. Yes there are many relevant people in our background, but you know what, the majority of them were plain ordinary folk who did nothing great or famous but just plugged away at life the best they could. Well the latter is my assumption as they don't feature in any history books, thank goodness! Phew, I didn't have to live up to these important ancestors or a Mata Hari mother. Unfortunately, I only became aware of the normalness of most of my ancestors in my late thirties when I took my second trip to visit relations and actually spent time talking about the past. Something I had formerly avoided like the plague as the past just seemed too much of a burden. We always had to live up to the family name.

The discovery that most of my ancestors were average was huge for me as for most of my life I remember feeling I could never live up to my heritage so actually didn't bother trying. I know for many such a challenge spurs them on, my brother being one it worked for, I believe, but I didn't feel I could compete so didn't try, a tendency I still fight today. All these strong achievers who did wonderful things in the face of adversity and me who not only wimps out at the first turn but wants to wimp out completely by dying. All calculated to make me feel even more of a failure. Why do I mention this? More or less as an aside to indicate that the grand achievements of others are not necessarily the spur for children some adults seem to think they are and to point out that some children give up under the pressure. They give up and so perhaps miss out on achieving maybe not great things but at least reaching their own full potential.

How can adults correctly gauge when to push and when not to? This is the sixty-four thousand dollar question but being vigilant of and receptive to the child's enjoyment or comments (negative and positive) is a start. Another solution is for those of us who do crumble under the pressure of too high expectations to manage to articulate this, something not easy to do as a child I admit but perhaps worth a try. As always discussion is paramount and may help both parties reach some neutral ground of relevant achievement versus lessened pressure. Not saying we should all give up, there is nothing wrong with achievement, it's just the level of achievement that may differ. Not all of us aspire to climb Everest, for some the local hilltop will do, neither being a greater or lesser achievement, and just because we don't aspire to Everest doesn't make us lazy. Who knows, having been encouraged to achieve our smaller goal, enjoyed the feeling of success from reaching the hilltop, we may have gained the confidence to try for Everest.

TIRED

Emotionally I'm screwed – the vortex again dragging at my feet to pull
me down.
I am weary of dragging myself up, only to have it lick at my feet again.
Its hunger for me consumes my will to live, my ability to enjoy life.
The ease of letting go is seductive.
Bliss.
No more pain.
No more struggling.
How seductive is total oblivion.

ASHES TO ASHES

What am I doing here?
I, who reluctantly stagger from day to day
am here
enviously watching them lower your coffin

Why you?
You, who loved every minute of life
was forced to reluctantly leave it
While I,
I, who would love to depart,
am not given that 'get out of jail' ticket

How I would love to trade places with you
but life continues its cruel game
taking you,
leaving me

NEW DAY

I choke on the new day
The sunrise catches in my craw.
How to stop this endless procession?

Yet another
          fake sunny beginning
bringing
          false hopes
          fantasy dreams

And yet
And yet
I fall for the illusion
every day anew

WHY?

Do I lack courage
Do I lack conviction
or
just
deep down
the real
genuine desire
not to face any more future

a meander through part of an episode of depression

What is life but fleeting moments of happiness,
strung together on a necklace of despair.

—*Marian Keyes*

I AM A 'SOMETIMES' DIARIST but find writing things down not only helps clear my thoughts but at times it is simply a reminder of things I want to look into, homework from sessions with my therapist, reminders of things I want to discuss with my therapist, revelations I have had, or just clearing of clutter in the mind. My various notebooks also contain exercises from whichever self-help book I may have been reading at the time, when I do them as that is not that frequent either. Anyway, here is a journey through a part of my latest episode.

Early March 07

The difference this time in my suicidal feelings is that I am not in some sort of pain. There is not one event that brought me to seriously contemplating death but a relentless wearing down by a myriad of small events.

Previously I have wanted to die, to escape pain as well as the feeling of showing them, but this time I just don't want to live. Why? I feel the desire is just that I can't see the point of it all, life is just *too hard,* it doesn't feel as if the reward/effort ratio is in the positive. I am sick of coping rather than living.

I lie here contemplating the meaning of life and why I should not kill myself, or else find a final rationale to do so!?

I live one life in my head and another, the one that others see, which are completely contradictory.

I feel completely overwhelmed by all that needs to be done to get my life back into some semblance of order and can't see the point of doing so.

Feel stuck with no options. When I do think of options I keep thinking of reasons why it would not work (fear?). Fear making decisions as keep thinking of all the wrong decisions I have made.

Need to look at:

What do I want?

What makes me 'happy'

What am I prepared to risk?

20 March 07

(They say that depression is anger turned toward yourself. I find it hard to be angry because as children we were not allowed to show anger. Hence this anger exercise.)

I am angry at Mum for not giving us positive feedback – for not praising us.

I am angry at Mum for making both of us insecure about our abilities.

I am angry at Mum for being perfect – not letting us see her mistakes or faults or slip-ups.

I am angry at Mum for making me feel fat, ugly, and unlovable.

I am angry at life for being so hard and painful.
I am angry at God for deserting me.

I am angry at myself for being so insecure and afraid and NEEDY.
I am angry at myself that I want/need love so badly but never believe
   when shown/given it.
I am angry at myself for not being totally self-sufficient in all respects.
I am angry at myself that I can't seem to find my bliss. I like everything
   and nothing.
I am angry at myself that I can't seem to find contentment.
I am angry that I seem stuck — know what I need to do but just hang
   there without the will.

25 March 07
I don't want to die, but neither do I want to live this life anymore.
But what sort of life do I want to live.
If only I knew?

   Surrounded
   Cornered
   Trapped
   by
   should's
   should not's
   must do's
   mustn't do's

   fear of showing
   vulnerability
   weakness
   needs
   wants

My much valued honesty a distant cousin to my need to be seen as
    capable, strong,
to be good – be better – be the BEST!

25 April 2007

I hate my need to please and be a good girl.
If I don't do what you want, I'm naughty.
Naughty equals unlovable.
I hate not being able to ask for things, fearing it makes me look weak,
lazy, ignorant.

My dream right now is to be free of worry about having to prove I'm
unwell and being able to just be. I appreciate people's concern but the
constant 'How are you?' is driving me insane as I have to put on my brave
face. This face hides the reality inside so no one believes I can't cope right
now.

26 April 2007

Am beginning to hate nights – spinning head, twitching body, restlessness.
Elusive sleep and awareness of the looooong stretch of twisted thoughts.
Want to be around people, they distract me and make me able to laugh,
but don't want to think.

3 May 2006

'I must have a project' suggests a friend.
Do I?
Am not pushing myself enough?
Should I force myself to do more?
Should I just let things flow?

Questions, questions, and more questions.
All without answers.
Is this madness I feel.

15 May 2007

Am excited, confused, fearful.

Visiting craft fair on the weekend invigorated me to be creative.

Could I find my passion there? Work for myself? And have my alone time but then convivial meetings at various markets?

Not have a job and regular income?

Would I be any good?

Could I make a living from this?

Sensible me – go to work, sell piece of land, and shore up some money. Take time to see if this craft idea takes hold, or just do lots of me work.

Naughty me – not work, hang out, do more work on me, as and when the mood strikes go to art school, or just be for a while.

Am feeling somewhat better but still no energy, still cry easily, still continue to walk through treacle. Feeling truculent about having to do anything. Want to be irresponsible and just play. But what is play for me?!

Touring around NZ and just doing what takes my fancy at any given time?

To not even think I *ought* to be improving myself/sorting myself out/ making decisions.

16 May 2007

I want to feel it's OK to just sit. Want to clear my mind of ought's/ should's.

To stop searching – let the answers come?

How?

Am I able to just be and let things flow as they will?

Really listen to my inner self (the child?) without judging, rationalising.

Short-term dream just go somewhere and be.
No cats.
No housework.
No friends.
JUST ME.

Feelings of guilt as
        I HAVE to be something
        I HAVE to do something
        I HAVE to keep in touch
        I HAVE to improve

But, do I HAVE to do improvement exercises to improve?
What is improvement anyway?

Seem to just want to hang out and get agitated when making real decisions
rather than dreaming.

Life wasn't meant to be easy.
Who says so?
Why wasn't it?

(I was not working, I had lots of time, and the opening lines of this W.H.
Davies poem is something that I often think of anyway; however, at this
time, they provided the seed for the following poem.)

        What is this life if full of care
        We have no time to stand and stare
                 —from 'Leisure' by W. H. Davies

I have time
But see only blackness
Dark alleys
Closed doors
A garden of decisions
One made
Another grows
Swamping me
As I fight through the undergrowth
It thickens ahead

17 May 2007

What factors most important to me?

BELONGING. If I belong, feel emotionally nurtured, the rest is (relatively) easy.

Tend to get very emotional in movies when friends, as much as family, are there through thick and thin. The ease of calling on one another. The being there for one another. The complete acceptance of one another. The feeling of understanding one another. The ability to be honest with one another.

INDEPENDENCE. Is this really important or is this part of my defence shield so I don't have to rely on anyone?

DOING GOOD – contributing in a positive way but also the ability to accept that I do so as when people say I add to their lives I dismiss this

WHAT WOULD I DO IF I KNEW I COULDN'T FAIL?

As at beginning of July 07
 move to the country (would I miss community/friends?)
 write/do crafts (would I be able to live off any earnings?)

enjoy cats, nature
grow own food
enter into a relationship/partnership

As at 10 July
Oh hell, reading this some days later now into being life/nutrition coach!

WHAT DO I WANT! ? ! ? ! ?

IMPORTANT NOTE TO SELF
Need to stop trying to force decision
Allow myself to be and experience. Decision will come.

Need some self-compassion.
But where to find it? Not available at the local store!

Trapped
I don't want to die, but neither do I want to live this life anymore.
But what sort of life do I want to live.
If only I knew?!

DAD – what I want from you?
Nicest thing you could do is find kind words and encourage me.
Being nice is more important than money.

Things to look at:
Anger – how I handle that
Assertiveness – how I feel about that
How I let myself know there is a conflict
Don't neutralise anger but allow me to feel it
The feeling of being an orphan
Track anger and disappointment

3 July 2007

The whole day thus far has been an exercise in FORCING myself to do the tiniest things and trying to evaluate how serious my situation is. Am I really depressed? Am I just lazy?

—*From Andrew Solomon's* The Noonday Demon, *page 95*

Examine:

Mum labelled me lazy.

Accept that Mum saw work differently.

To be able to cope with my difference she labelled me lazy.

I have achieved in my life!

I am physically and mentally active!

21 Sept 2007

I could by now do pretty much all of what I had always been able to do, except I was still in anhedonia – the inability to experience pleasure at all. I kept pushing myself for form's sake, but now I had the energy to wonder why I was pushing myself, I could find no good reasons.

—*From Andrew Solomon's* The Noonday Demon, *page 67*

Can't be truculent child now I'm well. Not allowed. Have to be responsible adult.

I am so tired, so exhausted of trying to figure out who I am when I'm fine – what is normal or acceptable for me?

Still struggling with self-praise. Must try to give myself compliments! As Lea (therapist) suggested, when I did some gardening tried to see what done rather than focus on what not done and/or still to do! Long way to go with this exercise!

Really just want to hide away in bed – not have to do anything but listen to radio. Someone look after home, cats, me. Sleep and wake (like Rip-van-Winkle) with all problems sorted and life going along well.

Every decision an effort and then the doubts flood in. Am I doing what is good for me? Am I doing enough to get well? Do I try drugs again? Could I have a better life if I did? Would my life have been different (better?) if I'd taken them years ago? How do I reconcile the outside with the inside life I lead? Does everyone lead this double life?

EXERCISE
If the child within could speak, she would say …
    love me Mum
    love me Dad
    don't tease me
    cuddle me
    don't put me down
    don't hit me
    don't pretend to be perfect
    hold me
    love/look after me even when I'm not sick
    notice me
    don't make fun of me
    accept that I don't make mistakes on purpose
    accept that sometimes I could have liked to lie in bed in the morning
        and not have to make your breakfast (and then have to sit and
        chat with you – I could have gone back to bed with a book)
    thanks for doing your best but not for the guilt that the bad parts of
        your life were our fault
    praise me not only my achievements
    praise/encourage me in my dreams not yours
    realise I am not showing off just because I show what I can do
    accept the need to ask does not mean I am stupid

One of the things I had to do to survive was ...
  keep silent
  not answer back
  not be loud
  not cry
  do well at school
  do as Mum said
  have no negative emotion
  be obliging

My fantasy is positive encouragement from both parents, not constant corrections or improvements or how I could do better.

HIGHER POWER/GOD

My God wouldn't expect me to work so hard to retain my equilibrium/ peace!

My God would be more visible — or make himself more known/felt to me.

He may be carrying me when there is only one set of footprints in the sand but I would prefer to feel him beside me *all* the time. Be aware of his presence without having to seek it.

This poem was written when I was out of the worst 'staring at the walls stage' of my latest depression, yet still struggling with life, death beckoning, but not having the energy to tidy and clean my home, write the suicide note and other instructions prior to taking the plunge. A state I seem to have been in for a long time now.

BOXED IN – ESCAPE?

I bounce off the rubber walls of my cell
No matter how hard I run
No matter how hard I push
        against these windowless walls
I seem unable to escape

Constantly crashing against the blackness

There is light out there
somewhere
or so I'm told
but
more and more
I doubt
its existence

The constant chatter
'Shall I?' 'How?' 'When?'
jangling my head
day and night
night and day
there is no respite from this lure of oblivion

Wanting to have everything shipshape
while not having the energy to shape the ship
Why bother?
Why leave everything as though no one lived here?

Inside of me
I am not shipshape
so why should my exit
leave no shape?
nothing for others to wonder at
to scrutinise
to criticise
to find fault with

No, I am not a blank page
I lived
even left a few footprints along the way perhaps
footprints washed away by time and forgotten memories
but still
they were there
albeit
briefly
as I was here
albeit
briefly

love! where is it?
what is it?

And for a moment she clung to him with all the
emotions of a frightened child, knowing suddenly and
with a terrible hopelessness that she would always feel
abandoned, even if it was she who did the leaving.

—*Doris Lessing*

I WAS RESPONSIBLE for Dad leaving. I was responsible for all of Mum's
misery. In fact I was responsible for so much misery in the world (yes
the world!) let alone our family no wonder I wasn't loveable. A feeling
emphasised by Mum telling me I was fat, ugly, and I would never marry
unless … well I didn't know unless what, but out of fear of this unknown
I became what she wanted to make me I suppose. So, not only was I an
emotional burden, because of all this misery, but I wasn't even pretty to
look at. What a *complete* waste of space!

So it comes to those years when suddenly you become aware of boys.
The romance novels take on a reality and the dreaming starts. Of course
fear of rejection meant I didn't openly admit I shared those dreams. I
didn't dare believe in them so imagine my surprise when suddenly I
became aware of the fact that someone loved me. I say became aware

because I had had boyfriends before, be they all very friendly and platonic and I can't remember why I thought that they weren't really interested in me. Perhaps because these boyfriends were friends of my brother I somehow put their apparent interest in me as a side-line to their friendship with him, they were being kind to their friend's kid sister or, as he was incredibly popular, using me as a way in to him.

In fact a recent catch-up with an old flame highlights how wrong my view of myself was and that he was as insecure as I was. Admiring each other if not quite from afar, we remained casual friends as neither had the confidence to advance. He remembered me as a statuesque beauty who he thought only wanted a pen-pal while I was visiting Dad in the USA. If only I'd known! I remembered thinking him too intelligent and good looking to be interested in a stupid ugly duckling. Yes, I accept some of these insecurities are just normal teenage angst but I feel they were exacerbated by my not feeling worthy of love.

Anyway, finally here he was. The proverbial prince. Not quite on the well-known white steed (actually a 50cc moped!), but hey the mode of transport wasn't important. All that mattered was he was going to take me away from all of this. Away from the wicked witch and off into the castle of happiness. However, before I really trusted him of course he had to jump through a few hoops to prove his love. Hoops that included a year apart while I went overseas to live with my father. To my amazement, he passed. He wrote regularly. He remained true to me. Most importantly he still wanted us to be together when I returned. To make sure he didn't escape, I asked him to marry me – against my mother's wishes I will add. I only add that to show I had to fight (and actually cajole *and* threaten) to get this prince. I wandered down the aisle with my very rose tinted glasses firmly in place. Now for the happy ever after. It was written in the books love conquers all. What a shock to find it didn't. Maybe it could have if I had had more trust in or understanding of it (love), but I continued to question any hint of a sign of rejection (perceived rejection?).

As with all divorce, this one has a myriad of reasons, but I'm convinced that my fear (expectation) of rejection certainly didn't help our relationship overcome the inevitable hurdles put in all our paths when we try and live with someone we love. In hindsight I can now see that in all future relationships I also ensured their demise by making the poor blighters prove again, again, and yet again that they loved me. Then there was the Catch 22 in that I didn't really truly believe their love. 'Leave before the rose dies on the vine', a line from a song (Carol Bayer Sager from memory) ran in my head and helped rule my relationships or the demise thereof anyway. The slightest hint of a lack of total devotion and I was off. Yes you heard right *total* devotion. I had to be number one in everything. Huh, you men weren't going to hurt me *again*!

When I separated from my husband, with it being the free loving 1970s and indulging in the free love concept, I began to sort of accept that maybe, just maybe, I at least had sex appeal. Although, in my defence, at the time I was not really aware that I used (abused?) the power in that appeal. Despite promiscuity being fun in and of itself, in the recesses of my brain I was aware that I was confirming myself, my attractiveness. Hey, someone fancied (perhaps even liked) me – even if only briefly. Having ensured I was good at 'it', there was the added bonus of unaccustomed praise. Also there was a freedom in not agonising over whether he liked me or not as in most cases I was not likely to see him again. All that mattered was that I, in that moment, felt love even if only in the form of a kiss, a touch, or some tenderness, in addition to feeling attractive, praiseworthy, and last, but certainly not least, in control. The encounters were mainly on my terms so there was little chance of my emotions getting a workout. Even if these feelings of being attractive, well, if not attractive at least sexy and praiseworthy, were only for small snatches of time, it was more positive time than I was used to! Not saying I didn't enjoy sex or that there were always underlying reasons for indulging in it, but even though I wasn't consciously aware of all of the subconscious motives at the time, I was aware of the different feelings between having sex and making love. Both enjoyable and with their place but different sides of the same coin, with having sex being the safer option as far as I was concerned.

For companionship I even entered the occasional short-term 'safe relationship'. Why do I say safe? Well I knew (believed) he did not love me in a forever sort of way. Anyway what he felt was less important as I knew I didn't love him in that way but he was comfortable and nice to be with and that would do for now. The chance of being hurt minimised by my minimal emotional involvement. (When young you have all the time in the world so spending months or years with someone not considered forever is a viable option.) In hindsight maybe their intent was different but I was clear in my mind so never really examined the level of their affection for me.

Where I hit rocky roads is when I fell in love and engaged in what I anticipated would be forever relationships. 'Me' went out the window. I became whatever I believed this person wanted. Being a doormat didn't stop me having opinions or standing up for myself, but my self-worth was measured in the mirror of his eyes. Of course I also continued to put the poor lad through all sorts of tests, each more difficult than the previous one, until eventually he failed. Hey presto. I was right. See. He didn't *really* love me! They say you ensure your expectations (negative or positive) are fulfilled and in retrospect I accept a lot of the responsibility for my perceived rejection, feelings that caused me to flee. It was the outcome I dreaded but it was an outcome I knew (ensured?) would happen. If nothing else hadn't life taught me that they always leave.

Yes, you guessed it, for now I live alone. As I said to someone recently when they were trying to pair me up, 'I don't do relationships well'. Despite all the learning and changing I have done, when I get into a relationship that means something to me, I still seem to fall into the trap of insecurity, fearing abandonment, and so I choose to live alone. As with everything in life, living alone has positives and negatives just as living in a partnership does, and while I don't discount ever falling in love again in my life, I admit for now that fear keeps me vigilant. Maybe when I feel secure enough in myself to ask myself 'Do I like them?' rather than 'Do they like me?' I will feel ready.

THE DANCE

Amid a flurry of noise
over enthusiastic laughter
they enter

To mill and circle
suddenly unsure what to do
poses struck

Affected conversation
Furtive glances

Subtle change of partners
the dance continues
inching closer
to the object of desire

Accidental contact
Feigned surprise
Animated conversation
The dance complete

| CHAPTER 7 |

food as love

If I let someone know I'm afraid of losing them, they will 'use' that fear to get away with things that are hurtful/ unpleasant for me. But if someone loves me surely they are afraid of losing me too?

—*Doris Lessing*

YEARS AGO I saw a Monty Python film, *The Meaning of Life* (from memory) and in it was a sketch where a man sat at a table with endless supplies of food. He ate and ate and ate and ate until eventually he exploded into thousands of pieces. Oh boy does this ever meet the grade for my favourite suicide scenario. Just imagine eating all I want of whatever I want *and* death at the end. What could be better! Damn and blast, it's just not viable!

How often did my brother and I lie on the floor in absolute agony? Mum having piled our dinner plates high and we had to finish everything. Even as a child I always felt this was most unfair. Let's face it she had served it. I accepted that when we had guests and I served myself, if 'my eyes were bigger than my stomach' it would be my stomach that had to pay. But when she did it seemed *so* unfair.

As a child Mum told me I was fat and ugly. This judgement did not stop her feeding us as if we were going to be the next offering to some deity. My brother's nickname for me 'Silly Running Sausage' didn't help my self-image (Silly Running Sausage/SRS – get it?! Alluding to the short fat British pork sausages not a slim-line frankfurter). Ha! Ha! Looking back on photos I see that I wasn't fat. The ugly part I'll have to leave for others to judge. The truth is that being an active child, playing lots of sports, my weight stayed pretty much the same for most of my youth. When I achieved my youthful weight later in life, people asked me if I was anorexic, not something that was talked about either when I was young. So I surely can't have been fat not having grown any taller in the interim.

As an adult I came to understand that feeding us was one of the few physical ways that Mum felt able to show her love – she was not a cuddler. One time, after realising Mum's method of showing love, and when she was visiting for a longer period of time, I managed to say to her that I realised that she wanted to show her love with food. However, as I was on one of my more extreme health kicks, I would appreciate her not buying lots of cake, chocolate, or such. If she wanted to treat me, she could buy me some balsamic vinegar, which I had recently discovered. Well when she left four weeks later I could have opened a shop selling balsamic vinegar but we were both happy. She could show her love and I could accept this form of love more graciously than chocolate where I would have felt she was sabotaging my health plan. OK I still would have preferred cuddles but had also come to accept that this was not going to happen.

Unfortunately, the realisation that I also show myself love with food does not stop me doing so. Comfort food! Huh, what a misnomer. Well I suppose it does comfort at the time. But as comfort foods are generally not the healthier choice, there is the inevitable weight increase. This then becomes another reason to dislike myself. Which leads to more comfort food. Which leads to … and so the cycle persists. Let's not go down the agonising emotional road of being weak added to the one of being fat.

To say I have huge issues with food is to minimise the problem. Food occupies my mind 24/7. 'What am I going to eat? When will I eat it? Where will I eat it? Damn, wish I hadn't had that … cake/chocolate bar/

take-out' or the 'Oh what a good girl I am' (when I have stuck to portion size and good food choices). Need I go on? These internal conversation variations are endless and those of you who share this problem will be all too familiar with the self-chastisement/praise seesaw we indulge in. The number of techniques I have employed in an attempt to control this uncompromising beast of continued emotional hunger seems able to douse its flames for a time but it waits, patiently, oh yes, it waits oh so patiently, for my next weak moment.

As you can see my relationship with food is very love/hate. Then there is this impasse in that it seems to be the only way *I* seem able to show *my* inner child love! But then of course I gain weight, which does nothing for my self-esteem. Both the physical self-respect as well as the emotional self-esteem becoming victims of this sick relationship with regard to food. Of course I don't like what I see in the mirror, but equally I *hate* my weakness in the face of food. But then feeling a failure turns my emotions to, you guessed it, food! And so the cycle grows an even longer tail. My saving grace is that I actually like vegetables, salads, and healthy stuff so I don't live on solely a diet of chocolate, ice cream, or greasy take-outs. *Big deal!*

Exercise and eating rationally, even while attempting to remember the 80/20 rule, is one of my biggest challenges, especially as I grow older. I accept, albeit with reluctance, that the solutions have to be lifelong, but it doesn't stop me secretly hoping that a quick-fix solution will be found!

My adult (over forty) life swerves in and out of sticking to exercise, going to the gym, sticking to the input/output equation to maintain health. The trouble is at the first sign of a dip in the roller coaster ride that is life and it's all forgotten. Then it's another long, slow slog back to some semblance of health and weight control.

Age doesn't help here with my real weight problems, as opposed to perceived fatness, only commencing after my mid-forties. Unfortunately as we grow older our metabolism slows down so we are supposed to eat less. Well I can't say I desire less food so it becomes even more difficult to reach and maintain a balanced weight, hence I continue to yo-yo.

Four years ago I got heavily into exercise and eating correctly, lost a lot of weight (got down to a New Zealand size 12/14 from 22/24, my biggest ever). Obviously, I felt great about this. So evangelical did I feel I even trained to be a fitness instructor so I could share my utopia. However, at the next emotional hurdle, what did I do? Once again, no prizes for guessing. Of course I turned to food.

Like a lot of my journey I continue to have more questions than answers around this issue. Despite reading many books not only on nutrition but also ones about the emotional addiction to food, my struggle continues. Oh yes I know a lot of the intellectual theory of how to lose weight, but it is the emotional side that keeps tripping me up.

Overeating is not the only dislocation of food and love, another angle of the misuse of food being bulimia, which later in my life is something I came to believe my mother suffered from. As a child I used to wonder at her trotting off to the toilet with her jug of water and hearing her throw up. I remember asking her why, as it happened nightly, and her response was that the onions and spices affected her ulcer and made her throw up. As she did the cooking I did wonder why she used these if they affected her so badly, but of course true to form I didn't voice this particular query. Some years later, having left home by then, when I was on an extreme diet I remember going to the toilet to purge when I had 'sinned'. Luckily I only did it three times before I decided that what went into my body was staying there. It wasn't until some years later that I even heard about this illness called bulimia and realised I had probably had a lucky escape. Some years later still Mum became terminally ill and the medication made her swell up. Friends came to visit. She became most agitated and distressed saying 'They only come to see how fat I've become'. Finally the penny dropped, Mum's 'ulcer' was probably bulimia. Although she fed her inner emptiness, and she had appetite, she also had to purge herself of this food to maintain her outward appearance. Perhaps it was her need to be beautiful that fed her need to make me feel ugly. Who knows but in my opinion love, food, and issues around beauty are hard to separate.

THE QUESTION

Dear Dad,
Did asking the question alter anything?
Does my me being fat change who I am?
Does you knowing why I'm fat change how you feel about me being fat?
What did knowing why I am fat change?
Did you want to ensure I noticed I am fat?
Did you want to ensure I noticed that you noticed that I am fat?

Why ask such a senseless question
about such a sensitive issue

Be aware
Most fat people are not fat because they want to be
The pain that leads to being fat
intensified by being ostracised from society

The only real balm being
Self-acceptance
assisted by
acceptance of loved ones

the gaping wound
in my heart

The secret of happiness is to be like everybody else,
yet to be like no one on earth.

—*Simone de Beauvoir*

THE GAPING WOUND in my heart that I tiptoed around and tried
to ignore was the space left by not having a father. My parents split
when I was four, and quite apart from the guilt I carried that it was all
my fault, there was an empty space. Well it wasn't empty as such; it was
a space full of pain. I don't remember my mother actually ever saying I
was at fault, but neither do I remember her saying I wasn't. Would I have
believed her if she had? Who knows? Why am I talking about this now?
Well as separation and divorce becomes the norm and I constantly hear
people say, 'It's for the best. The children will adapt' I cringe. The adult
logic accepts the statement. The hurt child wonders at its validity. Maybe
it is for the best for the two adults and yes in the end we children do
adapt, but at what cost? Let's face it, if you think about it, the children
have no choice but to adapt, especially when younger. You big people are
our only security. Where would we go?

The knowledge acquired later in life that most children of divorced parents feel they are somehow responsible has been an extremely powerful lesson for me. 'Hey, I'm not the only idiot thinking like this' and 'Hey Mum's misery wasn't my fault'. The 'If only I'd been better?' or 'If only I was smarter?' and the perpetual 'What can I do to make it good again?' put in their place. So, on the one side, I am sending out a plea to children to not feel guilty – it is not, never was, and never could be your fault. Reasons for adults breaking up are as varied as the personalities involved and quite frankly often not well understood by either party. The children becoming the flotsam and jetsam left bouncing between two, unfortunately often antagonistic, parties seem to be the price of the parents' freedom. Oh and by the way adults please note that we, the children, don't understand the nuances and certainly don't appreciate being used as weapons in your fight(s) with each other.

While begging children not to ruin their childhoods with guilt, I also ask parents to reinforce this fact, over and over and over and over. I would like to think that had I been told that Dad leaving and Mum's subsequent misery was not my fault some of my pain, perhaps even some of my feelings of being unlovable, might have been eased.

Or just not be put in the position of feeling I had to choose by having one parent, however obliquely, criticise the other. Even though Mum's bitterness was not focused expressly at Dad and she rarely badmouthed him directly, she was much too fair for that (!), however when she criticised men in general I took this criticism to read Dad and so I felt forced to choose. A choice I was unable to make. Being unable to make this choice, my lie of omission only increased my guilt. I felt a traitor and even more ostracised from family. Even though I never expressly said I did or didn't love Dad, the fact that I couldn't 'dis' him, couldn't side with Mum against men (Dad), weighed heavily on my conscience.

While there was anger at his deserting us, I couldn't hate him. My fear was too great that if I stopped loving him there would never be an option of him someday, hopefully, loving me. My dreams of reconciliation forever lost. Despite numerous times mentally cutting him off I believe

I have finally (at fifty-nine!) come to some reconciliation with and understanding of him. No, it's not hearts and flowers, too much water under too many bridges for that, but there is a measure of peace gained through understanding him a little more and learning that in *his* way Dad did love/ does love me. The message: Don't give up!

As far as my reality was concerned, I had no father. The one I did have being too distant in not only space but any contact to count. So as I wandered through life I picked up proxy fathers, i.e., any older man who was kind to me. When I could I clung to them, seeking approval and affection from them and generally, if only in my mind, adopting that person as my father. They never knew the burden they carried, and in hindsight I was probably a bit of a pain, but I would go to these surrogate fathers for chats, guidance, or just acceptance as in my imagination I went to my own father. Of course their own lives took them away, their family or work taking precedence, leaving me even more bereft, even more convinced that I was unlovable. However, not without hope as at the next opportunity I was trying again!

I don't wish to moralise that divorce is either good or bad. As with everything in life, there are pluses and minuses. We have choices. Choices have consequences. Consequences are experienced differently by each of us. The question of if it is better for children to be brought up in a home with two natural parents who are unhappy, arguing, or conversely in a home with one natural and one step-parent who are, hopefully, more loving toward each other, is better left to psychologists. I only wish to express this child's experience of this particular divorce.

Although experienced through my own filters and family history, I hope this gives children of divorced parents some insight and thus permits them to not only feel their pain and guilt but also to find the courage to express it. At the same time, I am also hoping to make parents aware that the adapted outer that the child portrays is not necessarily the inner picture.

Just because we have stopped crying.

Just because we have stopped asking 'When will Dad/Mum come home'.

Just because we seem to have accepted the situation (new parent? new siblings? new location?).

Just because we appear to have moved on, please note this is not necessarily the child's inner reality.

Face it, we have no choice but to adapt. You are all we have. You are our only security.

Having caused one parent to leave, we are certainly not going to take the chance of the remaining one abandoning us!

It probably needs lots of patience and understanding and though I wish it had been different, i.e., Mum, my brother, and me had been able to openly discuss and share, who knows what the outcome would have been if we had and if it would necessarily have been better? All I do know is that when I first went into therapy and would try to discuss my revelations with Mum, her usual reaction was defensive. The trick is to talk *and* listen without becoming defensive or angry, not taking things as criticism but just feelings. If only I had had the words at the time to let Mum know I wasn't criticising but just trying to understand her, her actions as experienced by me, to explain my side of things and perhaps be seen by her as an individual rather than a reflection.

A QUICK PRICK

A quick prick
A small injection
the serum thoughtlessly injected
the seeds planted
grow into beings

All remembrance of pleasure now gone
you turn your back on the consequences

Another must bear the brunt of your desire
fulfil obligations you created
attempt to give love you deny
yet herself incapable of giving something already given away
to you
so long ago the feeling forgotten
only the pain remembered

Two waifs
left
blowing in the wind
with no love to turn to
no security to be found
only the anger of her remembered pain
and then
with time
their own

WHO CARES

Who cares?
> Not the wind, hurrying along
> Not the sun, shinning brightly
> Not the sea, crashing on distant shores
> Not the river, rushing to the sea

Who cares?
> Not the mother, who left too soon
> Not the father, for whom she never existed
> Not the children, who were never born
> Not the friends, for whom she was an idle distraction

Who cares
> really?

| CHAPTER 9 |

the 'elephant'
in our family

Push truth down deep inside, it won't be denied.
At 3 a.m. it's back – bringing friends.

—*Andy Anderson*

I T WAS NOT UNTIL I was older that I became aware of the deep family history of depression and suicide. Lucky us! We had hit the jackpot as it was on both sides of the family. As they happened in my lifetime I could not remain ignorant of an aunt's suicide, nor a cousin's attempt, but apart from admitting that Granddad suffered from manic depression (I only learned recently that he actually attempted suicide four times apparently), Mum kept the rest hidden in her box of secrets. The knowledge of this family prevalence toward the black side of life and that this self-destructive gene seems to run in the family doesn't make it any less uncomfortable to live with. But I believe my feelings of alienation, of suffering this alone, of not being able to share believing I would not have been understood may have been helped if I had known of this history. The adult fantasy is that had Mum been able to talk about these things with me and help me take steps to minimise the distress perhaps my life may have been spent in less pain. Instead she denied this heritage, perhaps from her own fears or maybe the mistaken thought that if it were not spoken about it would not be real. Not every family has a history to draw on, but this does not mean that the black dog cannot visit any one of us.

> So much we run from
> So little we run to
>
> —*Mark Goile*

The constant struggle to find the sunshine in the day. The constant struggle to find reasons not to kill myself. Sharing these emotions and finding out that this was not some aberration. Finding out that this way of perceiving life could be if not normal at the very least acceptable and that it was possible to find ways to peacefully coexist with this monster. Would these discoveries have helped? Who knows? Would not feeling so different not only from others but also my family have been of assistance? From how I feel about myself and my guilty secret since sharing I believe it could have been.

I cannot change the course of my life, and who can be sure of the outcome if I could. However, I do believe the more these dark feelings are discussed and shared with those who don't have them, as well those of us who do, and as a result of this communication the feelings becoming better understood and less frightening, we who suffer from black moods and a desire for death will feel less ostracised from society.

The feeling of exclusion only adds to the burden, making death an even more attractive option. We the victims can learn ways to live with depression, learn what to do to stay healthy and what the signs are when we are heading towards the black hole. Parents, siblings, friends, colleagues can learn to notice the symptoms and perhaps with the courage of this knowledge feel comfortable to assist. Just like a diabetic realises they have to keep their glucose levels up, know what action to take if they feel they are slipping, but also many others now knowing what to do and feeling comfortable coping with any adverse diabetic situation.

We who have a tendency to slip into the black hole, tunnel (or whatever your version of Churchill's black dog may be), need to also remain vigilant, ensuring we do what we need to do to keep our happiness/survival levels up while also being aware of what we need to do when we feel we are slipping. Wouldn't it be lovely if we could be helped by those around having the knowledge to be able to offer assistance by understanding or just being there and simply accepting us.

During my latest black phase, I went to a neighbour and she asked, 'What do you want? Do you want to talk? Watch TV? Just sit? Or play cards?' The understanding and acceptance of me in my present situation contained in these options was incalculable to me at this time.

The first draft of this book completed, I was talking to an acquaintance. She asked how I was, what I had been doing. Although it was with some hesitation, I admit I felt safe enough in her understanding of depression to share and told her I had been writing a book and what it was about. 'How wonderful,' she said. For the briefest of moments, I felt good at being understood and acceptable. This positive emotion soon disappeared when she added, 'Now that you have got *that* off your chest, you will be over it and can move on'. For me the whole conversation now ruined. *'Don't you get it. I will never be over it. It is something I fight every day'*, I silently screamed while outwardly I smiled and moved on. Back to feeling misunderstood and feeling misunderstood leads to feeling unloved/ unlovable. Thankfully later I could accept she was trying to be nice, was being as kind and understanding as she knew how to be, but this event reinforced that people need to know more about this disease. It is not an illness we get over. It is not something we move on from. It is something we struggle with all our lives, whether we choose to arm ourselves with drugs or use other methods of survival or a combination of methods.

TEARS

Tears
held back for years
for centuries it seems
threaten to overwhelm my being

Yet
should I let them loose
would they ever stop?
could I survive
all the fury, and anguish,
they contain?

Or
being thus cleansed
what would remain
to seek a new day

Maybe this grief and torment
are part of what holds me together?
Does fear of the vacuum
prevent the tears?

THE END

A blank page
Nothingness
No pain
No sorrow
No doubts

'Ah, but you would miss the highs' say all

But in this game called life
The sands of joy and despair
fall upon the scales of time
not, as touted, in equal measure
but daily one extra grain falling
into the well of sorrow
into the well of pain
into the well of misery

Thus the balance
daily
tipping toward ...
        Darkness
        Why bother
        Agonising hopelessness

The mound of despair
gradually obliterating
the struggling rays of hope
blocking the sun
leaving only darkness

NOTHING IS IMPOSSIBLE

An ant
pulling a wasp across the path
unaware of the feat of strength required
to pull this object many times its size
only knowing this must be done
and
just doing it!

Inch by inch
achieving its goal
never thinking it can't
and so it can
and it does
just do it!

The human mind
supposedly our greatest asset
is often our greatest burden

Filled with constraining doubts and fears
instinct supplanted by logic
decisions in turn confused by choice
by notions of ability
by dread of failure
and thus
often
we end up
just
not doing it!

my four-legged companions and teachers

Pets are our seat belts on the emotional roller coaster of
life – they can be trusted, they keep us safe, and they sure
do smooth out the ride.

—Dr. Nick Trout (Vet)

IF YOU'RE NOT A CAT PERSON, you may want to skip this, but then
again it won't scratch you and you might even enjoy it! Come on,
cuddle up with yourself, your favourite stuffed toy, your dog, pet hamster
or rat, give it a try, and perhaps benefit from a different perspective.

Two bundles of joy
Weave their way into my heart
As they weave between my legs

Two bundles of joy
Weave a basket round my heart
As they weave round my legs

A basket of love
To shield
To protect
My self-love and acceptance

A basket of love
To cradle and nurture
The budding flowers
Of joy
Of hope
Nestled within

Daily weaving their magic
Making repairs
Strengthening the shield
Giving so much
Asking so little

—*Sinda Ruzio-Saban*

Cats are my present companions of choice. I have had dogs in the past but at the end of my last relationship I chose to have cats as I didn't want the responsibility of a dog when living alone. Cats provide me with unconditional love. Yes I know everyone says it is just cupboard love but at the end of the day, even if it is a premise I don't agree with, does it matter? Do I care? All I will say is that when I come home and they have a choice of food or a cuddle they choose the cuddle first so whatever their intent I feel loved over and above any food. Quite apart from the fact they also provide me with something to love, which seems to be as important to the human condition.

An added bonus to my love for them is the fact that, because I love them so much and of course no one else could ever love them as much or treat them as well as I do (!), on occasion my love for and responsibility to them has kept me going another day. I didn't want to leave them in the care of others and ideas of murder/suicide were discounted through fear of waking up to having succeeded with them but failed with myself. The other side of me remains sufficiently grounded to acknowledge they would make themselves at home elsewhere with ease.

My breed of choice is Siamese/Oriental, which are quite vocal so I can even have conversations with them. Conversations that are not too one-sided. Yes I am, almost, that crazy old spinster with her two familiars. I gain so much from them but like to think I add positively to their lives also. My choice is to have a least two so they are company for each other. At time of writing my cat family is three.

They seem to sense when I am not in a good space emotionally. One, unfortunately now in cat heaven, would sit on my lap if I was ever upset and while gazing into my eyes with utmost gentleness stroke my cheek. How can one not feel loved and cared for with that? How did he know I was upset? At the end of the day, it didn't matter, he was there with comfort. Or when I was bedridden for any length of time they would ensure that I was never left alone. They would touch noses at change of shift, one curling up with me while the other left for some timeout. The physical and emotional warmth is immeasurable.

A winter bonus is additional comfort in the guise of extra furry hot water bottles. Mind you, if I put the real thing in my bed, I have to admit they do tend to hog it, but I prefer to look on the bright side here and notice the additional warmth they bring.

Yes the downside is we outlive any animal companion and this is painful, but the joy they have bought into my life certainly outweighs this negative. And then there is the fun of the new kittens that bring such life and adventure back into my life that while the old are not forgotten the pain is lessened.

Taken from a daily reading of Al-Anon:

> I've given up the truth to those I've tried to please ... and now it's my turn.
>
> —*Michael Masser / Carole Bayer Sager*

> Sacrificing our rights often results in other people mistreating us. We deny our own importance if we say yes when we mean no. Saying no doesn't mean we reject the other person. It simply means we are refusing a request. Some of us become people pleasers and say yes to everyone and everything. We let other people, places, and things control our lives. We allow our personal freedom to be trampled on. We actually become numb to our own needs. Learning to say no is an act of love and honesty. When we speak up and are true to our feelings, people know who we are and where we stand.

During therapy it has been suggested I learn from my cats. The main lesson at the time was learning to say 'No' as well as not to take another's 'No' personally. What we can learn from our pets proved quite an interesting exercise and with this latest lot there are some new lessons. So here I share some of my lessons and if you choose to observe your pets I am sure you will find your own.

My first lesson was to learn to ask for what I want and not take it personally when I got a 'No' response. Easier said than done initially but over the years asking for what I want has become more natural with the feeling of rejection that automatically accompanied a no diminishing. I can't say I'm always able to just give my tail a quick flick as I walk haughtily away and move on but more often than not when I do get hurt

I am usually able to remind myself that it is not personal. Let's face it, how often do I say no? And it's not that I reject the person. It may be because I don't have time, money, or just lack the desire to do whatever. That it's OK to say no as well as receive a no is an important lesson learned. Back to our pets: Let's face it, the little blighters don't always do what we want either! At the end of the day, all going well, neither party (four- or two-legged) feels rejected.

Ahhhhh, that leads me on to admitting to not doing something I have been asked to do just because I don't want to. Saying no without feeling I have to give any reason. Talk 'bout scary! 'I don't want to' is that really enough of a reason? While still difficult at times this has been tremendously liberating. Which of us hasn't been in the space of giving a reason and the person coming up with solutions? 'I have a headache' take a painkiller. 'I can't afford to' – they offer to pay. And so it goes on until I gave in. There is nothing anyone can counter a 'I don't want to' with! Will they like me less? Well thinking of my cat teachers and looking at it from the other side of the equation, e.g., I want the cat to sit on my knee, coax, cajole, implore, bribe even, but if the cat is not in the mood – forget it! Do I like the cat any less? No. So why shouldn't that apply to human interaction? While I was constantly allowing myself to do things that I didn't really want to for fear of not being liked, *my* life walked away.

Is it worth it?
The half-lie
The compromises
The constant denigration of self

The 'It doesn't matter'
The 'I don't mind'

add up to
a life lost
—*Sinda Ruzio-Saban*

Recently I have again been reminded to look at lessons to be learned from my newest family members. One is insatiably curious, into everything, talks constantly, won't take no for an answer, and defiantly ignores any of my rules. You know what? I still love her! Oh what a fine lesson for me to learn; you can be naughty and yet still be loved. I get angry with her, I yell at her (she yells back!), and I spray her with water to try and teach her. She may react, especially to the water at the time, but continues the behaviour when I am far enough away not to be able to spray her. The bottom line: I continue to love her. Not saying I wouldn't prefer she didn't jump on the table when she expressly knows she shouldn't and I do get angry with her but, yes, I still love her. At present as I sit and write this instead of getting a nice secretarial job, my feeling of being naughty hasn't miraculously gone away but I am trusting that people will still love me for not doing as I *should*, i.e., get a job, any job, even if I hate it, even if I struggle with panic attacks at the thought. (Some months after writing this I did give in and got a waitressing job, despite the ongoing cost to both my emotional as well as my physical health. Just more proof that we are works in progress.)

My other new family member is shy, hesitant, scares easily, moving away to sit at a distance and watch life. Conversely, she is also the bravest at exploring when outside. A contrary mixture of strong/brave and timid/scared. My lesson from her? I realise that by being fearful, running away, and sitting just out of reach, she misses out on a lot of cuddles and love. As I do? Love she appears to crave, as when she finally overcomes her fear, she snuggles in so tight it feels like she is trying to curl up inside my body. Yes I scare easily reading rejection into a sigh, a raised eyebrow, or nothing at all at times it seems. I move away, become an observer, and thus remain out of reach of the love I so desperately crave. As she does. Yes I can stand up for myself in a physical way but emotionally I need to learn to trust, just as I am attempting to teach this cat. As she learns to trust my love, will I learn to be more trusting of others' love? This is such a *big* lesson for me. All I can say is, Watch this space!'

My latest addition is the smallest and youngest but that doesn't bother him at all. He won't die wondering that is for sure. Although he may pay lip service to the others' hisses and smacks, as soon as they stop he is back ready to play, fight, steal their food, or cuddle up with them. Not pushy, just persistent! And talk about cuddles. He is made to cuddle. I can carry him around, throw him over my shoulder, and he just purrs. Wherever I am, if he wants a cuddle, he just jumps up and places his front paws on my chest. 'Lift me up' say his eyes. Hard to resist. But the times I do resist he doesn't get offended or take it personally, to go back to the lesson of asking for what one wants and accepting a negative response without taking it personally.

I don't wish to suggest that cats are the only non-human creatures that can be teachers as well as excellent companions. However, because of what they have given me, I share them in the hope that you find some animal companion that suits your circumstance, disposition, and ability to care for, to love, to be loved by, as well as learn from.

Written to a cat of mine who seemed to be able to gauge my moods precisely and would stroke my cheek and remain with me day and night when required

THANKS KAIZEN

You sit
curled in my lap
gazing into the well of my sorrow
plumbing the depths of my pain

Slowly
almost hesitantly
your paw lifts
to gently
softly
stroke my cheek

"Fear not"
"Hurt not"
"I am here"
you say more eloquently without words

So much unconditional love
So much sincere tenderness
impossible to withstand
and so
I remain another day

Thank you

| CHAPTER 11 |

therapy – taking responsibility for my life

> All self-knowledge is knowing, on a deeper level,
> what one knew before.
>
> —*Doris Lessing*

| one-on-one therapy

The therapy I have undertaken has been of varied types and duration, undergone solo or in groups using Primal, Gestalt, Jungian, Clinical Psychology, Psychiatry, and Twelve-Step Therapies, either on their own or in combination.

Sharing with carefully chosen others is something I believe to be not only positive but essential. The very best part of this sharing for me is learning that I am not alone. Hey, my feelings were (are) not wrong! I was (am) not a bad person! The therapist's room was, and continues to be, a place where I feel safe and where I often still (at fifty-nine!) get to shut out the should's and find permission to be me.

Admittedly, I did not seek therapy out, it found me, and I can only say *thank you* to the Universe for delivering it to me. My initial opening up with a therapist was pretty much an accident. I was having a temporary separation from my husband. He had stayed in England and I was back in New Zealand. Well Mum being Mum wanted to know what the problem was, was it likely to be permanent, would I stay in New Zealand, etc., etc. The questions went on and on and as usual she was not getting much information from me. True to form she phoned my employers to see if I had spilled any beans to them with regard to what was happening. Anger had nothing to do with how furious and invaded I felt. However, as it turned out my boss was also a therapist (something I was not aware of) and with careful delving he unlocked my inner before I was really aware what was happening. I undertook therapy with him for some time and over the years have sought professional help from others at various times.

As an aside and I know the end result was good but this is an example of Mum's invasion of my privacy under the guise of 'I just wanted to help' that used to get me so angry and upset, quite apart from the fact that in this instance my employers had no idea that my stay in New Zealand was maybe temporary! Whatever, at the end of the day, in this instance, I am most grateful for the outcome, however I don't feel any less invaded. Therapy has helped me live a life not constantly wracked with pain. No, it hasn't been all sweetness and light since then, but at least there have been more patches of sunlight.

Quite apart from any empathy that may develop, a therapist is paid to hear my good, bad, and ugly. While I appreciate their lack of judgement and OK the cynical part of me thinks, 'They are paid to be non-judgemental', this does not diminish the immense value of their acceptance of me, the me that includes those deep dark hidden corners.

Even though I have learned to trust friends more, I still find it easier to open up to a therapist. On the other hand, after exploring my feelings and perceptions with a therapist, I often feel braver at acknowledging them with friends. For one thing, my emotions are clearer in my head and I thus feel better able to handle any possible negative reaction. Having said that, I do believe it best not to open to everyone willy-nilly. Sometimes it is safer to leave some doors shut and I continue to hide things I feel may upset people, things they might find difficult to cope with or things I feel (fear) they might not understand and where that lack of understanding may upset me more than the positive to be gained from being honest.

But the hardest part was that before being able to even attempt to be honest with other people, after finding out what I really felt, I firstly had to learn to be honest with myself with regard to my emotions, my motives, my desires. This self-honesty, though at times difficult, is the most liberating lesson I have learned, and if I am not really happy with the background reasons for pursuing a certain course, fearless honesty often helps me change my choice to one with hopefully a better outcome. If not better outcomes at the very least outcomes I continue to feel good about as they don't go against my own morality/ethics or inner voice.

For me my biggest evil was my thoughts of and desire for death. This feeling was strengthened by being brought up a Catholic where suicide is a mortal (major) sin. After many years of therapy, I was finally able to admit to certain friends, albeit in a very offhand way, that I had considered suicide; 'Oh but that is in the past', I'd say. This admission was only possible after I had come through an episode and was back to engaging with the world. With time I was able to confess that I had attempted suicide. With even more time and during my latest episode I was able to share these feelings while I was in the middle of them not only with my therapist but also with a couple of extremely understanding friends. (One is a psychologist and the other has had family members with depression so their understanding was optimal.) However even this sharing was not without coaxing from them.

I still feel weak for wanting death yet not doing it but, I found sharing my thoughts about my desire for it somehow lessened the pain of wanting to die. No, my desire for death didn't disappear overnight but continued to come in waves – waves that could be surfed with the help of these friends and therapy.

Recently, and for the first time that I remember, I was asked about details of how I planned to kill myself and discussed these. I was amazed at the relief I felt. Here we were, sitting in a café, discussing ways to commit suicide as if we were sharing a recipe or something totally mundane.

Laying my cards on the table helped shift something inside with regard to my shame and guilt that despite being eased is still operational.

In another recent episode a friend asked me how I was, and before I had even thought about it, and then wished I could reel *that* tape back, I had said, 'Really good. This is the second day in a long time I haven't had to find reasons not to kill myself'. We talked for a while about lots of things, not just suicide, and then when I was leaving, he just said, 'I'm here if you want me. However, if you do decide to kill yourself and succeed, know that I love you'.

These discussions and more importantly the implicit acceptance of my desires (me) are such recent events that I am not yet clear as to what shifted, if I ever will be, or if the shift will be permanent. Only time will tell. All I know is that for now I feel a lot freer around the subject. It's not so dangerous. It's not so shameful. They say you are only as sick as the secrets you keep? Is that it? These messy secrets are now revealed so it helps?

The thoughts and desires live on but I have finally found someone I can openly talk to about them and the peace that has come with that acceptance is indescribable. This person is a therapist, and while bound by the rules of disclosure if I get too high on the scale of desire to self-harm, is able while I lie in the middle/upper-middle range to allow me the freedom to bring bits of my desire and plans into the conversation without the whole conversation ending up being about death. For me there is the added advantage that this person is trained to deal with these sorts of things, is hopefully good at setting boundaries, and so I don't feel I am loading anyone up with panic thoughts of 'What can/should I do?' Suicide as **A** topic, not **THE** topic. What a relief.

Acceptance. Acceptance. Yes, acceptance really seems to be the biggest word around my thoughts and hence me. This normalising of my thoughts, the ability to share and not feel I am such a bad person somehow out of step with *everyone* has kept me going over the last months. As always I have more questions than answers and if this acceptance proves to be a permanent cure only time will tell.

One of the main things I have learned through therapy is to take responsibility for my life, my emotions, and how I experience the world. Sometimes I still rage against this responsibility. Let's face it, it was so much easier when I could say 'It's his/her fault', 'You made me feel/ do this'. Being a victim may be more painful but in a way it is simpler. Realising and accepting that I have choice in all that I do and feel is not always easy but it certainly is liberating. As they say, it may be simple but it's not easy! I am no longer a leaf at the mercy of any wind and blown along wherever it decrees. I see myself as more of a parachutist who may be blown along by the wind but by altering the canopy the parachutist (me) has some say in where she will fly and eventually land. Sometimes I still don't pull the right strings or just float but all in all there is great improvement and hence increased satisfaction in how I live *my* life.

I learned that my emotions are OK. Hey, I am allowed to feel angry, sad, happy. Ah, but it's how I choose to express these emotions that is important. I also learned that suppressing emotions only makes them come to the fore even more strongly. As one therapist said to me, 'They (emotions) want their time on stage and they will just wait in the wings until you let them have their moment'. Just because I am angry I don't have to shout and scream or hit anybody but I am allowed to feel anger. I am not bad for having the feeling of anger. Phew, emotions are neutral. Emotions are not good or bad in and of themselves; it's what we do with them that is important. I'm angry. I kill someone. Well I think we would all agree that is a bad act. However, I'm angry. I go into the woods and shout at the stars. Well I may be considered a little loopy but I don't think anyone would label that a bad act? Same emotion but very different expressions thereof.

Over the years I have been lucky in that I seemed to strike therapists who I liked, could get on with and trusted, with only a couple of mis-hits. I can't stress enough the importance of shopping around. I plead with you to do so and urge you to trust your instincts more than ever. Therapists are people too; they have their own demons and we have to like and trust them to be able to open up. Just because your best friend finds so-and-so great, he/she may not work for you. It is sometimes difficult to change, especially as when we seek someone out we are normally not in the best space, but I firmly believe however difficult it may seem shopping around for someone who suits you is worth it in the long run. At one time I ended up with two therapists for a brief spell. A friend recommended one. This therapist could not see me for some time and I felt I needed help *right now*! So I sought out another. For some weeks I ended up going to both until I could finally decide which one I felt I could work with better. It's your health and it is important to do what is right for *you*, not your Mum, Dad, friend, lover, etc.

While thinking therapy is great I don't believe it should be ongoing for the rest of your life. Personally, I delve in and out of therapy with my longest continuous period being three years. The way I approach therapy is that I learn, go out in the world to trial these lessons and new behaviours, and then go back for some more study. Unfortunately, I mostly end up going when finger-tip clinging to the edge of my black hole and even then I still sometimes leave it too late.

Waiting until the last minute means that when I first seek out a therapist I normally go weekly, very occasionally bi-weekly, for a time and then gradually taper off as I begin to feel strong in the world again. However, even when no longer attending regularly, with the therapist in the background I go into the world with the confidence of a child – the child who wanders off but knows Mum is there to run back to if it all gets too scary again. I know help is available but I have to seek it out.

For me a therapist asks the hard questions. They challenge me to honestly discover me and provide support as I try to live the new me that I am uncovering. They confront me. In the cocoon of a safe environment, they make me take a frank look at my motives, my way of interacting with the world, and let me find my own solutions to the parts of my life that don't work for me.

Even though my old patterns were self-destructive, they were familiar, felt comfortable, and were (are) at times scary and painful to change. However every courageous step makes the next one easier as I discover the world doesn't end because I say what I want, because I don't constantly acquiesce, because I have opinions. When I feel I'm being selfish, I concentrate on it being self-care. And sometimes I even have enough self-worth to think I am worth taking care of! (As I often repeat, I'm a work in progress.)

Therapists are better than friends in that they ask the awkward questions, which, to be honest, friends rarely do. Therapists make me find my own answers and solutions, which once again friends don't do as they try and help with their ideas. For me, if a therapist starts telling me what to do, I don't believe they are doing their job. Yes, they sometimes (rarely) make suggestions or give ideas, but the self-realisation, the final decision, is and must be mine. If I am not being challenged to answer my own questions, I begin to feel it a waste of time (and money).

Ah, while on the subject of money – try not to let the cost decide who you use. If it's not working for you, it doesn't matter how cheap, or expensive, the therapist is, it's a waste of money. What price do you put on your health?

Therapy is finding the answers from the past but taking responsibility for my present.

| group work

I have found group talking therapy work to be beneficial, but even just being in groups doing something of mutual interest can be helpful, although the self-learning is of course limited. For me the strength of working in a group is the realisation, yet again, that I am not alone in my thoughts and emotional responses. Horrible as it sounds, it is also extremely comforting to find that there are people even worse off than I am while at the same time it is most inspirational to look at those who have been there, done that, and come through it.

The ease of being honest with strangers is one of those things that just seems to happen and be beneficial. You know how it is sometimes, you meet a person whom you know you will not see again and suddenly you find yourself telling them all sorts of intimate things or visa versa. Well a group has often served the same purpose for me. Here are people who I won't necessarily see again after whatever period of time the group is to meet. As we are all there to learn about ourselves or new ways of behaving or living better in this world we seem to be able to be honest with each other in a way that doesn't often happen in the real world.

For me there is a difference between the weekend or ten-day groups I have attended where the possibility of seeing the people again is relatively small or something like Al-Anon where the likelihood of meeting the same people for longer is greater. Each type of group offers a different level of trust and sharing and I have gained much from both. Not only about myself and my sameness, but I have learnt to be able to give and accept criticism. Even more important though was learning to give as well as accept praise.

It is in these sorts of safe situations I have tried out risky behaviours with people from whom rejection would not have been devastating. Initially things as simple as saying no to a request that I could easily do or voicing a contrary opinion. When I first did this, believe me, it was extremely scary. However, I discovered that not agreeing with me wasn't a rejection of me as a person. Surprise, surprise, it was simply a disagreement with my ideas. Guess what? The earth didn't stop! Hence I became bolder about expressing (exposing?) the person I am inside. The biggest payout? I can agree to disagree now without feeling the world has ended or live constantly with the fear that the person won't like me if I have a different opinion.

Another benefit of my risky behaviour is that I can like people and continue to enjoy having them in my life but I can also enjoy them liking me. But, and it's a huge *but,* the big difference is that I don't necessarily *need* people to like me. I don't constantly have to jump through hoops for their approval. Not saying that I never leap through the odd hoop or two but it's a great improvement. As with all that I do, I continually have to accept that nothing in life is one hundred percent! Damn it! I'm not perfect, but the realisation is that I don't have to be perfect either – I'm just an ongoing project.

My Higher Power/God — Rediscovered through Twelve-Step Programs

For a good Catholic girl even living in my head was scary. God knew all my thoughts. Eeek! This God sat up in heaven and judged me harshly for any act, thought, or emotion not considered nice. In fact he was sitting up there in constant judgement waiting to stick these black dots of venial and mortal sins on my soul. However, having a black soul was better than being ridiculed by Mum, or even worse having my feelings disregarded, so I remained in my head.

Eventually I veered away from the hypercritical God of my youth and for many years only attended church at Christmas, weddings, etc. Luckily I fell in love with an alcoholic and through this discovered Al-Anon. I hear you question me saying luckily? Yes, luckily as through Al-Anon I discovered a Higher Power, whom, with time, I chose to call God. This new God loves me unconditionally. He sits up there on his fluffy white cloud offering a big soft knee to sit on and is ready with a cuddle whenever I call on him. The only trouble being I have to call on him and that is still difficult. Asking for help equates to being weak. Showing weakness is scary as someone may use it against me. So even with a loving God I don't always choose to ask. But when I do, the payoff is worth the risk and so I get braver with my trust. And even when I don't acknowledge him, he still loves me. That acceptance again, it's powerful stuff.

Then there is also the continual rehashing of the past or worrying about the future. I can't change the past and I have lost count of the bridges I have built and then there was no damn river! It is so easy to say and so difficult to do but living in the present is really a key. It is in these situations where trust in my Higher Power comes to the fore. My life becomes a lot calmer when I trust God, the Universe (or whatever entity greater than myself I have chosen to lean on), hand my problems, big or small, over and let God's guidance lead the way. Or trust that whatever has happened/is happening/will happen is right for me. To let go and enjoy today. Simple but not easy!

Changing Behaviour

As the Buddhists apparently say 'The only constant is change', I find it useful to remember that everything in life changes, from the seasons to the way I view the world and how I interact with it. So the act of my trying to control anything is counterproductive. Unfortunately, I can only control my own behaviour and if I'm honest with myself that is it! I can *attempt* to influence others but when they don't do what I think they should, when an outcome isn't what I wanted, what happens is that this failure to comply with my expectation leads to dissatisfaction at the least and anger as the other end of the scale. So it's best to stick to only attempting to change my own behaviour.

However, changing old behaviours is tough. It's a long, often painful, slog, but even with the odd backslide and repetition of lessons the outcome is so worth it. Although my old behaviours and patterns didn't always serve me well and the outcomes were more often than not painful they were familiar. Their comfort was in that I knew the pattern of the dance. I had learned how to handle the pain. In its way it was safe. The first few times I voiced an oppositional opinion or desire was absolutely terrifying. I started with what I considered to be simple things like stating a preference for a particular movie where previously I would have said I don't care, yet often cared desperately. Hey I had an opinion. What if they didn't want to see that one? What if they thought me silly for wanting to see that particular movie? On and on the internal dialogue went but I did it. And know what? The earth didn't stop spinning! They didn't laugh. They didn't reject me or my choice out of hand. Step by small step, I risked bigger, i.e., more vulnerable, bits of me, and as each step led to another, it became easier and with time almost second nature.

For me the 'I don't care' had become one of the worst things I could say as mostly I did care. It may not be earth shattering caring but I had preferences. I now always try to voice an opinion as I find it infuriating when both parties are saying 'I don't care' so not only is there a stalemate but consequently often neither party ends up doing what they really want. However, if I am genuinely easy about any alternate choices, but am just indicating a very vague preference because I want to avoid the 'I don't care' statement, I point that out.

Done all the hard work and got used to being honest and you know what? It doesn't mean I always get my own way. Who said life was fair, eh? Still sometimes I do and even if I don't the mere fact of voicing my opinions, ideas, desires, and have them listened to and at times accepted increases my self-esteem, my feeling of having some place in this world. Ah yes, lesson from my cats – ask for what I want but don't take it personally when I get a no.

| friends

Let's not forget friends who seem to come out of the woodwork when required. There are those who will run and hide but they are no less friends; it's just their demons won't let them cope with someone who isn't coping. I have continually been surprised at those people who do come up trumps and those who are less able to be there in this particular time of need. None is a better friend than the other, just different and I have learned to accept that not everyone can cope with depression (but I hope the more we learn and share the more people will be able to be there for one another). I have found 'black dog weather' friends in the most unusual places. Sometimes they just seem to appear for the duration of my need for them and then go back to being good acquaintances. At other times deep friendships have grown through this extremely personal period.

I have learned to accept what help is offered, even though I sometimes probably am not very gracious about it, as well as accept that some people won't want to know. My main difficulty is allowing others to assist me. The feeling of being a burden is often a hindrance to allowing people attempting to assist me so I have to focus on being open and accepting, most especially in my times of *big* need.

The same goes with sharing parts of my journey. I can't say I always get it completely right but with time I feel I have learned when, what, and how much to share with people. There are also different friends for different bits of me and hence the parts I share are as varied as the friends I have. Not everyone has to know *everything* about me, or even wants to I suspect. This continues to be the strength for me of talking to a stranger (i.e., therapist). I can tell them everything, no if's or but's. However, as I gain more trust in myself, in my friends, and in my place in this world, I find I am able to share more. For me the trust has to be not just that friends will cope but also that they will not gossip. Another plus of a therapist – they are bound by confidentiality so telling them everything is so much easier for me as I continue to be paranoid about privacy.

Much as I dream of being a hermit, I know I need companionship and the laughter and sharing with other people, but one of the hardest things for me to admit continues to be my need of other people's companionship. Having said that, one of my bigger realisations was when I finally felt I didn't need others, as in needing their constant approval, but of course continuing to enjoy having people in my life who like me. This awareness finally released me to be more open about who I am. Of course I love friends, socialising, and companionship, but I am less of a chameleon, constantly changing to be who I think they want. That is not to say I don't like approval and still sometimes fit in but it no longer is my only motivation.

Admittedly, aware of my neediness, I continue to be conflicted by the feeling I may be unwelcome and intruding in their lives but these days I often, but not always, check this out verbally rather than simply not going to them because I assume they have had enough of me. Sounds easy, doesn't it, just ask. Well I admit it's not always that easy but it is better than the alternative! The option of assuming they don't want me around and missing out on the company. Of course I have to trust their answer will be honest. The other option is that I don't go and visit but at least I now accept that it is my fear of their rejection *not* their actual rejection that is keeping me away, thus taking ownership of my part in this emotional conundrum.

My suggestion for you to use a therapist, especially initially, has to do with the fact that I found some friends were simply not able to cope with my dark side and I felt rejected when they changed the subject or suggested 'I get over it'. Such reactions caused me to retreat into my 'Everything's OK' persona, thus increasing the isolation even further.

This process of learning to live rather than exist is ongoing. How often have I thought 'I've got it' and slowly stopped doing the things that keep me as happy as I am ever likely to be until inexorably I slip, slide back to the edge of that black hole.

to medicate or not to medicate

This is such a personal decision that I have hesitated to mention it. I am an advocate for neither path. My decision to write about my view is that outside of hospitalisation, where you have no choice, my experience is that pills seem to be the first thing doctors suggest and it is not always easy in the depths of despair to feel one is making a good decision, if one is capable of making a decision at all. So my suggestion is try to give your view on medication some thought when you are in a good space. Research and do whatever you need to get information while you are well so you are armed when the black time comes.

In a way it was lucky for me that I stumbled on therapy before being asked the medication question. This gave me the knowledge there was another way before the pills option was introduced. It gave me time to think about alternatives and have an idea of what I wanted and/or felt suited me and my persona. Subsequently, I avoided medication where possible. My feeling being that medication only masked the symptoms, it did not cure and I wanted to find out the cause. In finding the cause I felt I was enabling myself to find ways to combat possible future episodes. There was also the fact that past experience had taught me that therapy helped me live my day-to-day more positively. Because of this, saying no to medication was made easier.

Because of my increased knowledge of the family history of mental illness, as well as the realisation that mental illness could have physical causes, during my latest brush with depression I agreed to medication.

Unfortunately for me it just seemed to exacerbate and prolong the deep phase of my depression. Then there was the added bonus of symptoms I have never had before: anxiety attacks, agitation, such a busy head that I was convinced I was going insane, the feeling of ants crawling all over my body and in my veins, as well as constant extreme headaches that would not budge with any pain medication, not forgetting the normal dry mouth, constipation. Need I go on? We tried different combinations, different strengths, and each had to be taken for some weeks before their final effect could be evaluated. This meant I was going through all these variations of bad phases for some time before it would be decided to try something else. Admittedly, I don't have much patience and so finally after a few trials with no real improvement in my condition, I decided pills were not for me. This decision was made not only because I felt like some sort of experimental guinea pig but I also believed they did not improve my down state. I was not experiencing the world any better nor was I any more able to cope than usual when I was well. All that happened was that I became paranoid about missing a day (this angst was even worse than when I was on the birth control pill!) or even taking any other sort of medication, be it a headache pill or vitamin supplement, in case it had an adverse reaction with the medication for depression and it all went to hell on a handcart. In the end I chose to go back to using herbal remedies combined with therapy and of course my tools (see next chapter).

While being aware that drugs are a wonderful assistant to many people I am not convinced they are the answer for everyone. In my case I did not seem to be physically attuned to them. I was told I am apparently extremely sensitive to their side effects, but was still encouraged to continue the experiment(s)! I admit I am psychologically not well disposed to drugs anyway so that probably did not help my feelings toward them, especially as they weren't the magic bullet we all crave. Where was my utopia?

I repeat I don't want to advocate for any solution, all I wish to do here is urge you to assess honestly how you feel about pharmaceutical drugs, how you feel if you take them, how you feel without pharmaceutical drugs, and not just end up taking them because the doctor insists on them or perhaps because the alternatives (therapy/exercise/etc.) feel the more difficult path. Unfortunately for me there doesn't seem to be a magic bullet, but whatever we chose, be it pharmaceutical drugs, herbal medicine, therapy, or various combinations, as far as I am concerned, it still takes effort on our parts to keep the black dog in its kennel.

(I am aware that there are mental illnesses where medication is the only solution; however, the above is my view on depression, which I believe does not fall into the category of a mental illness that is only able to be treated with medication.)

BE – LONG - ING

I am longing to Be
be part of Something
something Greater
greater than me

Me inclusive
Inclusive not Exclusive

However
Exclusivity brings safety
   a probability of pain

Inclusivity means risk
   a possibility of pleasure

I am Longing ...

toolbox for maintaining my serenity

OVER THE YEARS I have collected a set of tools that help me. This is of course providing I not only actually use them but also choose the right one for the job at hand. As with life, the process is ongoing. How often have I thought 'I've got it' and slowly stopped doing the things that keep me as happy as I feel I am ever likely to be until inexorably I slip, slide back to the edge of that black hole.

Here is a selection of what my toolbox contains (in no particular order):

- Maintain an *Attitude of Gratitude*, trying to look at what I have rather than what I don't. Be grateful that I have been able to notice that bird singing, enjoy that sunset, or a myriad of daily small happenings, from being reminded to stop for milk just as you were about to sail past the shop to being made aware of the danger ahead early enough to enable me to avoid that major crash on the way to work. These small pointers keep me in the here and now, not agonising about past mistakes or worrying about bridges that haven't even been designed, yet alone built over nonexistent rivers.

- Watch my vocabulary with myself, attempting to get rid of should's, have to's. Accepting that if I haven't done something, for myself or someone else, saying it is because 'I didn't *make* time' keeps me aware that it's not that I didn't have time, no one stole it, I just didn't make time for whatever, that there was something else I gave priority to. Through these inner dialogue techniques I stop being a victim and through losing the martyr role I reclaim my life.

- Daily readings – from various affirmative or twelve-step programmes' books

- Meditate – spend some quite time with myself and do my best to clear the brain. This is not necessarily sitting cross-legged on a hilltop 'Ooooming'. It can be as simple as playing gentle music and focusing on one instrument. In fact I have found this concentrating on one instrument an excellent way to clear my mind. Years ago I read a book, *Meditation for Everybody* by Louis Proto, that discussed all sorts of ways to meditate and made meditation accessible to me. Today an equivalent would probably be called *Meditation for Dummies.*

- Listen to relaxing music/sounds – some CDs have forest streams, ocean sounds, birds. It doesn't have to be exotic wailing from another culture but whatever you enjoy. Classical and Gregorian chants sooth me equally as well as some New Age music. Whatever works for you, however, keeping in mind that the latest rap isn't going to exactly have a calming effect.

- Exercise – physical as well as mental, i.e., go for a walk, go to the gym, but also taking time to read something challenging or instructive. I have spells of voraciously reading self-help/improvement books, be they for emotional, fitness, nutrition, or motivational purposes. I also have times when all I read are chick lit or detective novels, not to make me out like some kind of saint.

- Eat well – I don't have to be a bean-sprout-eating health food junkie but the emphasis is on trying not to overeat and ensure a good supply of vegetables and fruits as well as portion control. Must admit I am lucky in a way as I love vegetables and salad so even when I am on a chocolate/chipies binge, fresh food is maintained in the diet. My tendency to overeat being a bigger hurdle than my sweet/chipies tooth.

- Sleep – I need *at least* eight hours and now accept that this often means going to bed earlier than others but I have to weigh up what is important for me – being thought a wimp or my equilibrium.

- Socialise – I need to have contact with people. But need to be aware that contact on the phone, or these days by computer, while helpful is not sufficient to fulfil this need. I need to be physically in their presence, to see their faces, breathe the same air, and be able to touch the other person.

- Ask – When hurt, I try to check out with friends if they meant what I heard; this is especially important as one false interpretation can set me back down the slope. However, this continues to be incredibly difficult, even though most times what I have heard has nothing to do with what the other person meant.
  'Hey, when you said that, I felt … Did you mean to hurt/upset/ ridicule/…/… me?'
  'Are you aware that I felt hurt/upset/ridiculed/…/… by that?'

These are some of my solutions. You will find what works for you. The knack is to find those two or three things that if done daily offer the most help in maintaining a positive attitude, the rest being an additional boost to your well-being or alternatives for swapping to and from. For me I know the Attitude of Gratitude and Self Vocabulary are my main lifelines. The Attitude of Gratitude keeps me not only focusing on the good things in my life and the world but also in the here and now, while the self-talk helps to prevent me slipping back into being a martyr, buffeted by others' choices with no chance to make my own decisions.

Now of course it is all very well filling your lovely toolbox with these bright shiny tools, opening it every so often and admiring them. Unfortunately, the trick is to use them! Of course I don't use all of my tools all the time. But to be effective the main ones do need to be used regularly. Over time I have learnt those that are the bedrock of my serenity, and I attempt to use them every day. However, I also check the toolbox every so often to be reminded of what other help is available. Different strategies seem to work at different times. Sometimes I do something for a few days and then grab another tool. Other tools I use for months on end. Also I am always on the lookout for new ones.

However it is easy for me to get carried away and want to use as many as possible, especially when I am coming out the other side of a black phase. I have to remember that for me this is counterproductive as it only adds stress in that I am not doing *everything* possible to get well as invariably I can't do all the things all the time.

Sometimes as I slide down the slope to blackness despite all I have learned and the subsequent changes I have made to my behaviour I forget to open the toolbox and select the tool more appropriate to the particular situation.

There is also the risk of becoming complacent when life is chugging along OK, minimising the tools' importance to this feeling of well-being. I feel good so I forget to use any and, oops, I begin to be aware of my feet sliding from under me, eventually.

Initially I was quite upset when I figured out that I would need to be vigilant for the rest of my life. However I have come to accept that there will never be a time when things will just be fine for me without having to do anything. It doesn't mean I don't sometimes feel it unfair but unfortunately maintaining my serenity is a journey not a destination. Just like readjusting my eating habits to lose weight. Having reached my weight goal by eating sensibly and regular exercise, I can't simply go back to being a couch potato feeding my inner child junk. Maintaining a goal weight is a lifelong commitment as is maintaining my mental health. I will never be well and thus I have to commit to using the tools on a regular basis, forever! This daily commitment is incredibly difficult and not one I manage all the time. Bad habits seem to stay impregnated in the cellular structure of my body but the good ones need a lot of work to even get going and then some of them need continual vigilance so they don't run away. Damn it, it's not a perfect world! And I'm not perfect! Double damn!

> Perhaps is always forever
> Always is perhaps forever
> Forever is always, perhaps
>
> —*Mark Goile*

There is no time where you can be complacent with the tools of your choice as I found out with my latest brush with depression. I learned the necessity of choosing *the* tool for the job and to *not* just reach in and grab any. Having been reasonably stable for some time, I knew it all, or thought I did. Hence, as I became aware of the black cloud approaching, I continued exercising (getting up at 5 a.m. to ensure I could), I made a point of socialising so as not to isolate myself, and I spent money I couldn't really afford trying to fix some of my ongoing physical problems in an attempt to minimise my physical pain. Yes I was doing things I knew were good for me. What I didn't take account of was that I was going through a time (menopause) when sleep was constantly elusive so getting up early was not such a good option, that I tend to worry about money so spending large amounts no matter how good for me added stress, that my normal work was going through a difficult time and I with it while at the same time I was trialling a new career where I constantly felt inadequate (stressed). On reflection, getting up at 5 a.m. to ensure I exercised every day and doing a lot of socialising when I was not getting much sleep were probably not the best tools at this stage in my life, no matter how good the intent. Nor was spending money on physical help that not only prevented me from seeking out mental help but also added to my worries and stress as I watched my bank account decline. So it's not as simple as figuring out what tools work for you, it is as important to think about which ones you use at any given time. As I discovered, what worked last time did not work this time. Yes, it is difficult to listen to your body as it is sliding down the slope, but all you can do is give it your best shot. Don't beat up on yourself if you don't get it right, as I am determined not to do.

For me power walking regularly and doing my affirmation(s) are ongoing supports. A reminder that an affirmation is always in the positive as you are reprogramming your mind, or trying to! Initially for me there is often a huge internal argument, but you know what, eventually the brain no longer fights the new information. However it seems to me that some of the reprogramming is more difficult for the brain to retain so I attempt a constant reminder by using the jingle below regularly. This to remind myself that life is a choice as well as reinforcing the idea that it is a celebration. It is my favourite and I do it for at least half any walk I do. Hey, I even sung it to myself when I trained for a half-marathon and I'm no speedster! This latter comment just to indicate that for me the number of times I sing/say an affirmation is not an issue despite most books I have read recommending to repeat it a certain number of times in front of a mirror or whatever. Not only does this jingle remind me to be positive; it also stops my mind from dwelling on the negative and doing that wonderful circular thinking we can get into.

(Sung, or quietly thought, to the tune of Row-row-row your boat, taught by Susan Smith at a health conference, though not sure if she is the author of the words.)

I choose to live my life as a celebration
Healthfully. Joyfully. Peacefully. Lovingly
Life is but a choice.

For me, if the affirmation is too long, I forget it so I mostly tend to make them short. I think the rule-breaker above works because of it being set to music, although it is not excessively long either really. Often

I read long ones in books and if I think them appropriate for me I break them down into parts. But mostly my affirmations are tailored to my needs so feel it best that I compose them.

This takes me to the second half of any walk that is mostly taken up with a self-composed affirmation on an issue I am working on at present. They have ranged from:

I enjoy having a flatmate and we are having a good time together. (To be honest this was one of my less successful affirmations but it worked for the time I needed a flatmate. However, as soon as I was financial again, well let's just say I was happy when she decided to leave.)

to

I choose health. I enjoy power walking. I love going to the gym. (This took a very long time for my brain to accept, especially the gym bit, but guess what? Eventually I got to the place where I did enjoy going to the gym and exercising!)

Note: Sadly during my last brush with depression my affirmations fell by the wayside as well as the exercise and now I am back to the beginning. This just to, yet again, affirm 'It's never over!'

As stated above, my internal language is also important. I try and stick to using 'I *choose* to do/be'. Doing this keeps me aware that I didn't *have* to do whatever, it is my *choice*. I don't *have* to go to work. I choose to, as I want to maintain my lifestyle. I give this example as it is one that has had the most impact on me. Years ago I was listening to the radio and the subject of choice came up in the discussion. I remember the person saying 'but I have to go to work?' with the announcer (or whoever) saying that even that was a choice. Yes, if you chose not to go to work, you may end up under the bridge in a cardboard box, but at the end of the day this is still your choice. My mantra now is that *Once I'm born the only thing that I have to do is die, everything between is a choice.* Of course, with choices come consequences and it is a matter of weighing up whether the consequence is worth the choice! And sometimes having made a choice that leads to a consequence I didn't think about and don't like, accepting it was my choice, my decision, not someone else's fault, helps me feel less disgruntled and make an alternative, hopefully better, decision. Oh yes, I have finally learned that I am allowed to change my mind, i.e. change a decision. Also very liberating.

| CHAPTER 13 |

hope / dreams / courage

> You cannot live on hope alone, but without it life is not worth living.
>
> —*Harvey Milk*

'I F A JOB'S WORTH DOING it's worth doing right!' Which of us hasn't heard that refrain. Mmmm, being perfect is not merely hard but in reality is impossible. That notwithstanding I judged everything I did by this standard and unfortunately continue to fight this critical inner voice. It doesn't matter how many people tell me I shouldn't be so hard on myself and much as I'm better able to be kinder to myself I actually often don't notice I'm being harsh until someone points it out.

I've been wallowing in my latest miasma of depression for eighteen months now and I just don't seem to be able to find motivation for anything. My much vaunted tools sit there, quietly in their case, waiting to be of service. I may pull one out for a day or two but it soon loses it lustre. All I see is a future of conformity. Conformity to job expectations. Conformity to fiscal expectations. Conformity to life expectations. Expectations that no longer feel mine but expectations to which I don't see a viable alternative at this stage.

Don't see? Oops, well maybe it is just me being afraid of that leap into the void! OK so I'm no longer merely motivated by what I feel I should be doing, i.e., getting a decent job and going back to the life I have lived. Conversely, there is also wanting to be sure whatever road I take is right, that if I take this risk, it is what I really, really, really want. However, as I say this, I realise I am sitting here writing this, fulfilling a long held dream of sharing – a sharing that I hope will help others. Finally, doing this giving me a reason to get out of bed. Writing this also helps fuel my dreams of being able to sustain myself in a less structured, more creative way. Whatever the outcome, it adds wood to the fire of my dream to allow my creative and caring side to develop. It gives me courage to see what the future could hold. As the song goes 'If you don't have a dream, how are you gonna make a dream come true?' Oh but the fear of stepping outside the box. The fear of failure overshadowed by the fear of not feeling any more fulfilled at the end of it all. *Then* where would I be?

Bland. Bland. Bland.
Oh what was she doing
allowing herself to be part of this?

This colourless landscape.

She lost her own vitality
She blended in
and
eventually
each colour-matched day
equalling a new death

—Sinda Ruzio-Saban

Although I have travelled, lived in other countries, and spent time not necessarily living what many would see as a straight-laced life, let me tell you all the extrovertness was highly constrained by what I felt was decent, acceptable, and above all the need to live a good life. Was it my life, I don't know. This is the first time that after getting over the worst part of my latest depressive episode I have actually taken time out to just be. Yes I feel compelled to look for work. White-collar work of course. To fill the expectations of …? Are these expectations mine? Are they my mother's? Are they society's? Whose expectations are they really? There is also the guilt of not being a good girl, not doing what is expected of me (again I ask by whom?) and hence reaching back into that unlovable space.

When I left school Mum sent me to a tertiary school to learn to be a secretary. 'It's a skill you can use anywhere' was her advice. And yes it has proved useful in getting me jobs around the world. But for the most part I have felt like I was in another skin. In interviews when asked what sort of company I wanted to work in, I always said I didn't really mind what I did, it was the people I did it with who were more important. As I examine this statement now, I realise it probably is more indicative of the feeling I had about my actual work. The job, the tasks involved, were a means to an end, i.e., money to live my life as well as living up to perceived expectations, but what really mattered to me was the people, the interaction(s), the companionship. I was one of those children who actually liked going to school. Was this also because I enjoyed the companionship of friends there? I often joke by saying 'I still don't know what I want to be when I grow up'. At fifty-nine doesn't that sound a little sad. A life lost existing. I suppose the positive of that joke is that I am still open to exploring new avenues. At fifty-nine I haven't given up!

For years I admired (and envied) an uncle of mine who at age forty changed careers to become a potter and became successful at his craft. He had a wife and two children so it surely took courage to take this risk but whenever I saw him he was extremely happy. I continue to be inspired by his example whilst still not having found the courage to step outside the box.

> People often end up doing what the mirror tells them they are suited for, while feeling themselves quite different inside, and in the process, whole lifetimes are thrown away.
>
> —*Alan Bennett*

After being well (as far as the outside world saw anyway) for some time and feeling pressured to get back into society, I took a job. Office work. It's safe you see. I didn't like the job quite apart from having anxiety attacks each morning just at the thought of going. I told a friend I was not happy. Her response: 'Well at least it's getting you back into a routine'. It was only when she said that that I began to *really* question why I had to be in a routine. A routine of society's making. Was it mine? Was it what I wanted? Finally I couldn't cope so left this job and yes I admit to still looking for jobs but right now it is taking more courage *not* to work, to just be, and attempt to find out what my bliss really is. Not that work has been my whole life but I also realise it has provided me with an identity. People don't ask who you are; rather their first question is, 'What do you do?' Is my profession who I am? It seems a long way from the dreams I hold inside. Dreams crippled by fears of inadequacy. Fear of going outside the norm. Fear of failure. Fear of not knowing enough, of not knowing how to do it properly, of not doing it well enough.

> I hesitated, held back by that fear of ridicule that had
> paralysed my childhood.
>
> —*Simon de Beauvoir*

Yet again the road to self-realisation and fulfilment seems not only rocky but difficult and painful, but experience has shown me that the journey is worth it. Although I am also quite sure that once I have conquered this challenge the next awaits. Part of me wails, 'Not fair', however more often than not each successive hurdle becomes progressively easier, the landing is not as harsh. Each lesson building on the last so the legs (soul/intuition) are strengthened for the next leap. Although I also now accept that some lessons need to be learned a few times before they sink in. I remember once angrily saying to a therapist 'But I thought I had learned *that*!' Her quiet response: 'Well every so often a Universe just sends us a little test'. Not that I'm particularly enamoured by that concept but unfortunately life has taught me that this seems to be how it goes. The mean part is you don't even get grades to know what you've passed! However I have a longstanding friend and we have gone through many extremely rough patches together. We now take delight in pointing out when either of us has responded or acted naturally in a way very different from what we used to, i.e., *that* lesson stuck! The trouble with lessons learned, because they become second nature or *normal* behaviour, we are no longer always aware of the positive impact. Fair? Who said life was fair!

It is such a cliché that hope keeps us humans going, but like all clichés it has truth in its depths. Apart from hope, I also need to find a purpose, even more as I age. This is where I now sometimes wonder about my choice not to have children. I don't regret this decision, but I wonder if at the dog end of life it gives a reason to put up with the almost inevitable physical pain, the invisibility of age, the external ageing of the body that I am experiencing? Not that children stay around, as both my brother and I lived at the opposite end of the globe from Mum, but does having that self-created individual to worry about and care for give life meaning?

SOLITUDE

Solitude.
Wonderful.
Blissful.
Quietude

Crickets begin their evensong
An occasional bird squawks goodnight

Leaving only the husssh of the waves
blown by the gentle wind.
Constantly moving forward,
driven
to crash upon the rocks
to lap against the shore.

God created this symphony.
God created me.
I can see and enjoy this harmony
Why can't I see and revere me?

HAPPINESS?

What's this?
a curious feeling

an unfamiliar
hesitant guest

the fleeting hint of sweetness
swiftly overridden

the bitter conquering
drowning
any chance of pleasure

CHAPTER 14

the good bits

Thinking against oneself often bears fruit; but with my
mother it was another question again – she lived against
herself. She had appetites in plenty: she spent all her
strength in repressing them and she underwent this denial
in anger. In her childhood her body, her heart and her
mind had been squeezed into an armour of principles
and prohibitions. She had been taught to pull the laces
hard and tight herself. A full blooded, spirited woman
lived on inside her, but a stranger to herself, deformed
and mutilated.

Her love for us was deep as well as exclusive and
the pain it caused us as we submitted to it was a reflection
of her own conflicts. She was very open to wounds –
she was capable of chewing over a reproof or a criticism
for thirty or forty years – and her diffused indwelling
resentment made itself apparent in aggressive forms of
behaviour – brutal frankness, heavily ironic remarks.
With regard to us, she often displayed a cruel unkindness
that was more thoughtlessness than sadistic: her desire
was not to cause us unhappiness but to prove her own
power to herself.

—*Simone de Beauvoir*

N OT ALL that my mother did was bad nor do I wish to suggest that it, my misery, is all her or anyone else's fault. When I first got into therapy, I used to ask her about events and emotional responses that I'd discovered. She would get defensive, say my memory of the event was incorrect, or even deny it happened. Gradually I realised that it was not good to attempt to talk with her about past events and their impact on me. With time (age) and more understanding of myself, I allowed Mum her reality, realising that I wanted people to allow me mine. I no longer tried to make her not only see it from my point of view but also make her accept that this is the truth. I came to understand that truth mostly lies in our hearts, our experience of events, and not in the actual events themselves. My brother and I often joke about the fact that we may have lived in the same home but were brought up by a quite different mother. Although there are a lot of memories that are similar, or even the same, much of how we experienced Mum is diffused through our own emotional filters, needs, wants, and hence very different.

While I accepted that any backward look at our life was not contributing to any present harmony, I did begin to sometimes have the courage to check out today's reality. For example, one time she was visiting for a longer period and also staying with me. I had recently become a vegetarian. For days she kept on about people she knew who were vegetarians, about how they looked weedy and how they were always sick. On and on and on and on. I experienced these comments as criticism of my choice, as I often had with similar things in the past. When I finally got the courage and challenged her on this, i.e., why she always had to 'pour cold water over anything I did, believed in, or was enthusiastic about', her response was that she didn't mean to sound negative and was only concerned for my health, was worried, etc., etc. I accepted her explanation, her truth. The main positive, quite apart from letting my feeling be known, was that thereafter she became extremely supportive.

Another constructive spin-off from this conversation was that some of the old hurts – hurts that unfortunately I also have a tendency to chew over for years – got given a different filter. I didn't discuss these old wounds with Mum, but by checking out this recent event and examining our differing reactions, I was made more aware of how my negative reading of past events may also have had a completely different, and possibly positive, slant if seen from Mum's, or Dad's, side of the fence.

PERSPECTIVE

Points of view
are just that
nothing more
nothing less
not right
or wrong
or good
or bad
just another way of looking at the world.

You look at if from your perspective
expecting others to see your view

Yet they stand on another hilltop
walk through another valley

Have you ever thought to go there
and look at it from their side?
—*Sinda Ruzio-Saban*

Ultimately we all have our own demons we carry with us. My choice to break the chain of misery I felt as a child was not to have any children, a coward's way out perhaps. Over time, with therapy and the deeper understanding of myself, and hence I like to think a better acceptance of others, I came to believe that every parent does the very best they can. Yes that does include those who end up bashing or even killing their children. I don't deny that in these cases their best is worse than poor but it is the best they can do with the demons *they* carry. There are, I believe, very few truly evil people. Few people who set out to destroy the lives of others. With this understanding, it has been easier to forgive the perceived transgressions of my parents. This knowledge doesn't necessarily stop me being upset, hurt, or probably taking things the wrong way, but when I tap into my belief that they did and are doing the best they can, it helps diffuse the pain. Even better is when I take the courage to check out what they meant, be this with parents, friends, and even co-workers at times.

At the end of the day Mum had her own demons and I firmly believe she gave her life for us. Unfortunately, her love was overshadowed by duty and by the need to keep outward appearances at all costs. Despite the pain, I can't say it was a bad life. We always had good food (albeit too much at times!), a roof over our heads, physical as opposed to emotional warmth (i.e., warm clothes, heating), and we were given as much assistance possible to pursue our studies, hobbies, and/or sports. Only in hindsight am I aware of what sacrifice this must have involved for a single parent; at the time I was only aware of the times 'we 'couldn't afford 'it'. That the child may have wanted love shown differently does not take away the fact that she loved us, cared for us, and protected us to the absolute best of her ability.

A lovely memory of the protective side of my mother is from near the end of her life when perhaps being older myself I was able to appreciate it more too! Anyway we were on holiday in Bali and on the first day I had bought something from a shop that we ended up passing on our daily constitutional. The walk wasn't far as my mother was not well at the time. Anyway, on each subsequent walk, the shopkeeper would shout my name, follow us along, haranguing me. I became very cross at this harassment and was muttering to Mum about how this woman really annoyed me. True to form, I did nothing but mutter. Suddenly, this frail old lady, who had been hobbling along all hunched over, rose up to her full height, turned, and told the shopkeeper in no uncertain terms to stop her harassment of her daughter, to leave her daughter alone, etc. After which Mum slumped back into herself and we continued our walk as if nothing untoward had happened, which in hindsight probably for Mum it hadn't. But here, to me, was a very practical demonstration of her protective instinct towards us, her love for us, her way of protecting us from all the bad that she could. Which brings me to the statement I made earlier: 'She gave her life for us'. I am convinced that all that she did was done with our good in the forefront of her mind and she used up her inner resources to do so, hence her relatively early death.

However, just recently I was made aware of the fact that although I now can temper the anger and pain of my youth with an understanding of the good side of Mum, I am left with this huge guilt. I made the statement to my therapist that 'Mum gave up her life for us. Just like Christ she died on the cross'. As I said it, tears formed and on examination I realised it was that in my heart I feel guilty. Guilty for not recognising her sacrifice sooner and guilty for that fact that she did give up her life. She was with us or running her business, had little social life of her own, and worked day and night to provide what she felt important for us.

For some years now I have felt good about seeing Mum's nurturing side. It was a positive that I could finally see the good side of her and negate the damaging element, not realising how destructive the thought of her giving up her life for us is for me. It sounds nice. It sounds forgiving. Hey 'She was a good Mum in that she did her best, which is all one can expect, right?' But when I said she was like Christ and died on the cross for us, well admittedly it still took a therapist to guide me to the realisation that maybe she wasn't quite so saint-like and how this view may add to my guilt at not being nicer to her when I was young, or just my general guilt at being alive and her not. Mmmm, apparently it is now time to attempt to marry the two images of Mum and get a whole person. Neither sinner nor saint. Work, work, and more work!

Dad was distant, emotionally and physically. Not only did he live half a world away but communication in those days (the 1950s and 1960s) was extremely difficult. Phone calls? Well the phone connections were not only expensive but by simply standing in the backyard and shouting one would have probably got a clearer line. How to write letters to someone one doesn't know? Not helped by his humorous responses when I did write, which hurt as I did not feel I was being taken seriously.

The first time I spent any length of time with Dad was when I was seventeen. In retrospect probably not the best time for either of us to get to know one another. Those prickly teenage years no doubt only adding to my feeling of being misunderstood. Over the years and after some hurt, real or imagined, I often mentally turned my back on him, saying to myself that this is just too painful and I don't even want to try anymore. However given time I would crawl back like a dog, its tail between its legs, with just the tip wagging, hopeful. Until the next time of pain. A cycle oft repeated.

As mentioned previously, it is only recently, at his eighty-eight and my fifty-eight years of age, that I have felt reconciled with the person who is my father. I can accept him (mostly) for who he is. I still may not always like his humorous responses to things I consider serious but then again neither would I want to lose the humorous side of him. We don't agree on all things. But it is no longer *as* scary to disagree with him.

All in all I am aware that this is who he is, as well as and more importantly, being able to accept he means me no ill when being funny at a time I don't appreciate, in fact the complete opposite. During my last brush with the black dog, he was so supportive and kind, hey, he even gave me some praise. Praise that I had never heard; if he had given it in the past, I haven't heard it. In fact the only praise I remember receiving from him was that I always got a good job – see what a good girl I am!

Some things he did recently still bring the happy tears to my eyes and finally I am able to recognise that he loves me. How exciting is *that*! I finally can look back and see the examples of his love and have at last been able to spit out *some* of the cud of the times I felt unloved, that I felt he considered me a blight on the landscape, cud that I have chewed on for years. Yes I admit it is early days and I still tip-toe around him a bit but I have opened up a little of my dark side(s) and not been rejected so it gives courage to open a little more. As in these things it's step by step, slowly, slowly, catchy monkey. Progress not perfection.

The following poem was written many years ago. With my recent, hopefully better, understanding of my father, I can now look at it and give a wry smile. Mmmm, maybe I should have been writing it to me, from Dad's perspective? Did I only look for (see) the bad? How blind have I been? As mentioned previously, although late in life, I have finally made peace with both the sinner and saint of my father, so I add this poem as I feel it says as much about me as it does about him.

DEAR DAD,

So easy to find
the faults
you so earnestly seek

Luckily
friends seeking the good
remind me of my humanness
and
halt the devastation
of your fault finding

Poor Dad
What joy you could have
in me
if you chose to
look for the good
but you so earnestly need to be right
so desperately need me to be wrong
that you miss
the positive

| CHAPTER 15 |

a mother's blame pain

WHEN I SHARED various drafts of this book with friends and fellow sufferers, I got positive feedback. Friends who were perhaps happy to nosey around bits of my life I had kept private. All very lovely and confidence boosting but then came the question of how it would affect someone who did not know me? To test these waters, the latest draft of the book was given to a friend of my brother. As my brother lives in the States and I in New Zealand, any knowledge this friend had of me was limited to a by-line or two from my brother. He chose her as a critical outsider because he felt she was forthright, outspoken, and courageous in her utterances. At the time my brother was not aware that her daughter suffered from depression so her input feels even more valuable.

Having written this book from the perspective of a person suffering from chronic depression and mainly attempting to help others in this situation, I became aware in her response to the book how much this illness can affect others around us, most particularly parents. Not only did this mother gain insight into her daughter's pain but also was able to let go some of her own. Like all of us, what we have not personally gone through we cannot understand, so to realise what an effect the black dog has on parents was an eye opener for me. To be honest, I never thought of parents and friends suffering, as she has so clearly indicated, but was more focused on us poor depressives (selfishly).

But to know this book can also reach out to others and shed some light (particularly for parents) in the way it did for her feels just awesome.

These were people who I had hoped to educate about our suffering without thinking of (or realising) theirs.

Her email made me aware and want to point out that as much as I harp on that children should not feel they are responsible for their parents' divorce, unhappiness, or whatever, neither should parents feel responsible for their children's depression. There are so many factors that can play a part in being and becoming depressed and the bottom line is at some point we all have to accept we are and can only be responsible for our own lives and our own choices.

Yes of course parents play a part in making us who we are, as do so many other outside influences along the way, notwithstanding the fact that we experience the events and world around us in a personal way, expressing this truth in how we live our lives. However, at some point, the child, or perhaps adult if it takes longer, needs to accept that they are responsible for making the choices and if they don't like the outcomes it is up to them to make different choices. Don't blame Mum, Dad, society, unfairness of life, etc., etc. – it is now up to each individual.

> Life is not the way it's supposed to be. It's the way it is.
> The way we cope with it is what makes the difference.
>
> —*Unknown*

Taking responsibility for my life has been the most painful, difficult, liberating, and exhilarating thing I have done. That is not to say I don't still sometimes lash out and want to blame God, the Universe, or anyone I can grab hold of, but the bottom line is as much as past experiences, and my perception of these, may have added to the mix of who I am and how I act (react), whether I allow the past to rule me or not is now my choice.

So until now you've looked inside the mind of a chronic depressive. Here take a peek inside the mind of a mother of one.

Dear Sinda,

It has been almost a week since I spent the day reading your most awesome book, and have thought of little else since. Although I do run with the black dog from time to time, it is my twenty-one-year-old daughter who is more affected by the darkness. And me as well, as her mum.

Could you possibly know the anguish, fear, panic, sadness, exhaustion of trying every tactic and solution to "solve" my daughter's lack of energy, blaming, blackness, mood swings, screaming fits, lethargy, anger, hatefulness ... If she would just change her outlook, take a yoga class, finish college, take vitamins, quit smoking, get more exercise, go for that promotion, etc., etc., THAT would make her happy.

If I hadn't said that, if I hadn't pushed so hard, if I'd been there more often, been more understanding, less bossy, more giving, more together, hadn't divorced, my daughter would not be depressed.

It is my fault, you know! That's the game, blame myself, while saying and doing every wrong, unhelpful thing that pushes my daughter further into her black hole.

But now I know ... thank you, that even what I perceive as encouragement is not helpful, and even hurtful for a person who is fighting the battle. And thanks to your sharing, I am learning what may be more helpful, and that pointing out for the millionth time that my daughter is lazy is NOT constructive!

And the sad fact is that maybe there is nothing I can do to solve her problem ... But I think now I understand that it is what it is and that we will learn and experiment together on what may turn out to be a lifelong quest for wellness, and I am not to blame nor am I going to find that instant cure I think I am responsible to find ... I am crying again ... This is so painful ... I know I would rather be depressed than watch my daughter suffer. And I am sure it was the same for your mum too. How generous are your conclusions about her and her own struggle. I hope someday (soon) my daughter will come to understand that I will do anything to help and support her and that her suffering is mine as well. And that we all (it seems) suffer from the anxiety of our shortcomings, and berate ourselves for our imperfections. Especially moms!

My conclusion from your book is this ... This is our journey, be what it is. We will carry on and work on it day by day ... It may not all be solved today or tomorrow, but that's OK and we have not failed as long as we keep on the path. Stumbling and falling are part of the process.

Sinda, thank you for sharing your book with me. It has helped me enormously, as it will others when it is published and out there. Stay the course and be well.

Fondly,
Holly

| CHAPTER 16 |

DEAR DREW

So you did it
You finally did it
It was the third attempt I hear
Was it third time lucky?

Lucky for you
       perhaps?

The end of your pain
       perhaps?

The end of the
agonising
tortures
of the
mind
       perhaps?

Unlucky for those left behind
Left behind to mourn the loss of
your smile
your laughter
your smell
while discounting
your anger
your tantrums
your moods

Me.
well honestly Drew
I knew you too little
to mourn more than
the loss of a young life
the loss of your hopes, and others' hopes for you
the loss of your dreams, and others' dreams for you
now, not even given the chance to be realised

However, I must admit that
while mourning
the loss of a member of the family of the human race
I,
at the same time,
cannot help but wonder:
'Have you found peace, on the other side?'
'What is really there, on the other side?'
'Is it really final, on the other side?'
'Is there even, an other side?'

And I?
Well I cannot help but envy
your courage
your tenacity
and yes
even your final success

Dearest Drew
May your peace be final
and may we
who remain
find peace in life

Although this poem was written as a form of eulogy for an ex-partner of a good friend of mine, it sums up my feelings about life and death. Because of my preoccupation with the pain of life and the escape of death, I do wonder what it is like on the other side, or quite frankly if there even is one. The Catholic in me wonders (worries) about hell and purgatory, the spiritualist queries the possibility of an afterlife, another side of me hopes for total oblivion. Which is correct?

The whimsical part of me does find it interesting that Drew succeeded on the third attempt. 'Mmmm, third time lucky', so as to my question: Was it really lucky? Would I really be better off dead? Do I even genuinely prefer to be dead? As a friend of mine said recently, 'Well you're still here, so it can't be all bad'. Which is true. Although part of me envies Drew's courage and success at the end of the day, the truth is that life isn't all bad and like a drowning sailor we (I?) treat the passing bits of hope as lifesavers.

I sincerely hope that when I do die, be it by my own hand or naturally, there is peace. In the meantime my sincerest wish is that I, and any fellow sufferers, continue to find contentment here on earth. If not continuous happiness that we at least get sufficient glimpses of it to keep us carrying on. Alternatively that we retain sufficient curiosity to see whether those eighty-plus-year-olds who say it only gets better are right?

Each day has a dark and a light period. As each life has a dark and a light period. The trick when sitting at the bottom of the dark hole is to remember that the sun will rise again. As it will no doubt set again. And rise again. The bad passing just as the good does. A truism I (we?) oft forget, of course especially when it would be of most assistance to remember!

So, enjoy the sun but remember to dance in the rain.

With love.

POSTSCRIPT

A S MY MAIN MOTIVATION in writing this book was to get people to talk about suicide, I feel it behoves me to be open about some of my latest insights and frustrations.

As I continued luffing in the dark with no light in sight I planned to have this final section of my book only if I proceeded to take my own life. However, as time goes on, I feel some of the frustration (anger? questions?) in this section are worth sharing so have decided to include it either way.

It is now 2010, more than three years since my last fall from grace and never have I struggled so long to get back on top. Yes I am functioning but not in any way I recognise. I freak when I go for jobs, I find less and less reason for anything I do, and just can't get back into life. The things everyone says to do that will make me feel better only make me feel worse and then I feel even worse for not getting better! Somehow, through the strong family genes perhaps, I manage to pull myself together enough to show a functioning outside but the energy this takes means that most of the time I am too exhausted to do much else. Is this life? Is this a life I want to live?

However, as I ponder, in essence I have been a good girl for the last three years, even when I was being what I perceived to be a bad girl. Being a bad girl meant not doing what I thought was expected of me by family, society, i.e., not working, not cleaning the house, not cooking healthy meals, but mainly just reading and hiding away. I felt I kept being naughty by not doing what I thought was expected of me. Ah but the crux – I continued to think I ought to do what the voices keep telling me.

I felt I should be living up to their (whose?) expectations and felt even more of a failure in that I didn't. The other side of this is that although I felt I was being a bad girl and was living with this guilt at the same time, I was really being the good girl by trying hard to find joy, a reason to live, and using your solutions not to let you down.

If I do end up killing myself, this final act comes not out of a sharp shock of pain but is more due to the long, agonising, extremely deep pit I have lived in for the last three years. A pit that sometimes, for brief moments, I have managed to lift my head slightly above, but never managed to haul myself out of. The simple truth is that I am weary, my mind has given up trying to find reasons to live. I feel I have searched hard but I can't find any good reason to keep up appearances. The emotional pain, increasingly aided and abetted by the physical pain, exhausting.

Whether or not I have managed at last to find the courage to kill myself, this section is my plea to all those in authority to listen to *my* madness, *my* uncertainty, *my* fears. Listen to *me* as *I* am experiencing these and not through your filter of what is best for me. Admittedly I don't necessarily know what is best but being submerged in *your* solutions isn't my answer. The tiredness of depression exacerbated by constantly wondering why your answers aren't working yet feeling I have to fit into your mould to gain assistance thus leaving less energy to trial my solutions.

If I am dead by my own hand when you read this, you may feel killing myself is too contradictory. 'Huh after all the fine words in this book with her solutions and helpful hints, she killed herself in the end anyway so what does she know?' However, all I can tell you is that all the insights and lessons I learned along the way and shared here have made my last forty or so years not only bearable but even enjoyable at times and they have brought me this far in relative peace, but they are not a blanket cure.

| are pills the answer?

The following may appear to be an attack on doctors and medicine, which at some level it is, but at another I really want to highlight the difficulty (aloneness) I have felt by not being able to share my deepest (sickest) feelings with my medical practitioner. I know I have said previously that honesty and sharing is extremely important and I believe it to be so. However, when the sharing leads to your prime (only?) solution of medication, and you refuse to hear my fear of pills, secrecy, lies, and increased feelings of isolation follow. When the doctor said to me 'When are you going to accept that you will have to take pills for the rest of your life' was when I shut down for good.

> HEAR ME
> pills
> your solution
> my agony

What I experienced as the guinea pig approach of try, try, try again until something works (even if only sort of) led to the prescription of a plethora of medications with side effects, including melancholy. There was the reality of constant headaches (take a pain-relief pill), continued insomnia (no problem, here are some sleeping pills), and constipation (there are pills for this too). It was considered more acceptable being treated with pills than listening to my anxiety around medication as a long-term solution and perhaps together seeking other answers. I feel that if I want your (i.e., the doctor's) help, especially with the paperwork for financial assistance, I must take pills. There's also the threat that if I don't take the pills I either won't get any help or alternatively I can be legally forced to. Who listens to the person for whom pill taking of any kind is anathema? Surely there is a place in society for looking at other solutions? Let's face it, the trial and error method of pills is not necessarily a quick fix, so other long-term solutions could be looked at for us pill phobics!

Questions only, I have no answer, but surely if your aim is to keep us alive, alternatives to pills and coercion may be worth looking at as long-term solutions?

As I examine my pill phobia, I wonder if it is a consequence of not being allowed to fail? Everyone tells me pills are the solution and the crux of the matter is I can't get fiscal help if I don't take them. But my problem is that I just can't seem to go there – mentally or physically. While perhaps not taking pills may well be hindering my recovery, I just don't want a pharmaceutical crutch. I don't want to be dependent on pills for the rest of my life. Let's not forget the added paranoia about the possible (negative) effect if I miss one. A lapse that feels more scary than missing a birth control pill ever did! Also even when I was taking them (oh not for long enough I hear you shout), I got no further than this state of existing I am in now but of course there was the added bonus of their lovely side effects as alluded to above.

Going through the motions on the outside but feeling trapped with nowhere to go on the inside. *Help* – I feel I can't share my real wish for death with anyone. This anyone unfortunately includes therapists. This is not meant to be critical of any therapist as they have been instrumental in assisting me to make my life liveable but it is anger against the system. A system that in effect does not allow us to be totally honest with our therapist as they are required to report us to authorities (authorities = doctor) if we admit to being on the verge of suicide. A doctor. Mmmm. A doctor trained to give me pills. Pills. Mmmm. Pills, the taking of which only increases my negative feelings. And so the cycle deepens.

I note that often suicides are attributed to people who have stopped taking their medication. It is also said that they stopped taking their medication because they felt well. What is not taken into account is that with or without pills after passing the initial really dark phase I never felt any better with medication. My suicidal feelings and desires, my inability to cope with any setback (perceived or real), my lack of energy did not improve further. The only thing the pills seem to do for me is give me a constant headache.

Instead of listening to me, I got vague threats: 'You refused medication' (to which I hear 'So why should I help you with the paperwork?') and 'When will you accept you have to take meds for the rest of your life' (when I had started to taper off as I did not feel any better).

So perhaps people stop taking their medication because, like me, it has not really helped and taking it is mentally/emotionally more destructive than the depression – not forgetting the negative side effects, which are happily glossed over in the quest for an apparently healthy (subdued?) patient. I will emphasise that I am not talking about all 'mental illness' here as I am fully aware there are some who can only be helped with medication nor am I trying to dissuade anyone from taking medication if it works for them. I have friends who have found medication helpful and are happy to take them till their dying day. I am only attempting to point out that there is another side to this particular coin.

Who says I was coping better with meds? Or is me being better simply your perception? The number of times when I have been hanging on with fingertips to the edge of the pit, people have come up to me and said, "You look so much better now that you … are on medication, … have found a job, etc." They see what they want to see.

is work the solution?

'Get a job. Get back into the swing of things'. Another mantra heard frequently. We'll ignore the stress of applying for a job when everything freaks one out, when every rejection letter (or non-response) feels like a knife to the chest. Finally having found, and got, a job, there is the anxiety that builds for days (not hours) prior to going, the energy required to hold it all together while there, and then the total exhaustion that precludes doing much else. And these feelings not just on the first day but *every* time I go, and it's only a waitressing job! Of course when I mention my problems, there is the 'You'll get used to it'. For now I'm not so sure.

Yes, I manage to get it together to go to work, to meet with friends, and then comes rest, lots and *lots* of rest. And you know what happens then? Oh yes, my good old friends, guilt and shame come calling. It has been some months now and I can't say I have got used to it, but the good girl continues doing it. Perhaps you are right and it will finally become a positive?

self-talk

Work:

Klutz you can't even do a simple waitress job right.

You are so stupid.

Schheee getting all worked up about a stupid waitress job.

Jeez you're an idiot?

You REALLY are a waste of space.

How can you be exhausted, the job isn't THAT demanding, and let's face it, it's only two nights a week. Get real.

Home:

Do I like living in a mess? No.

Do I feel good about leaving dishes for days? No.

Do I feel good about not cleaning my home for weeks? No.

So perhaps I feel good for spending money I don't have, if only for a moment? Nope THAT doesn't work either.

Well on take-out then as am too tired to cook or on junk (comfort?!) food and watch my weight creep up?

No. No. NO!!

Rest:

Don't be so lazy.

YOU'RE exhausted!!!

Exhausted from doing what?

Get up you lazy bum and stop feeling sorry for yourself.

| others' perception

'You're looking *so well*. Oh, I can tell having a job and getting out and about is doing you a power of good'.

I smile and walk on. Tears of anguish and shame at still not feeling that way, tinged with the incomprehension of others of my agony. Tears to be shared with my cats and shower.

What is my solution at this time? Honestly, I don't know yet. What I do know is that authority's solution isn't working for me, nor are some of my old tools, but the search continues.

But wait, there's more!

For those of you who may feel they have been touched, inspired, informed or even annoyed by this book and want to talk about the book and/or it's contents I have set up a blog page.

Please remember that those sharing are human beings with feelings and I ask you to be at the very least respectful of each other and opinions that may differ from yours but hopefully you'll be supportive and thoughtful.

Enjoy.

thebitinbetween.blogspot.com

www.ingramcontent.com/pod-product-compliance
Lightning Source LLC
Chambersburg PA
CBHW060852280326
41934CB00007B/1010